REACHING FOR THE LIGHT

A PATH FOR DEEP HEALING, FORGIVENESS AND RE-EMPOWERMENT AFTER SEXUAL TRAUMA

By

Petros 'The Human G.P.S.' Galanoulis

Foreword by Sarah Monahan

Author, Advocate and Actress - *Hey Dad*

**Join Us For Exclusives In
The Reaching For The Light Facebook Group**

Share your favourite parts of the book

Your inspiring story

Support

Great interviews

Insightful and exciting videos,

Events,

Competitions,

Specials plus more.

www.facebook.com/groups/reachingforthelight

Warning/ Disclaimers

The material in this book is of an adult nature and may be too graphic for some. Reader discretion advised and guidance for young adults is suggested. The events in this book are real life events that happened to the people in this book.

One name has been changed to protect the identity of that person.

This book is offered for educational and general purposes and is not designed as a replacement for professional personal counselling.

Thank you.
Petros Galanoulis

Reaching For The Light:
A Path to Deep Healing, Forgiveness &
Re-Empowerment After Sexual Trauma

Cover design: PurQua Design Studio (purqua.design)

Layout and Typesetting: Working type studio, Century Gothic size 12

Published By: Petros Galanoulis, Melbourne, Australia.

Printed by Ingram Sparks.

All enquiries to www.yougotthismentalhealth.com.au/contact.

REACHING FOR THE LIGHT

A PATH FOR DEEP HEALING, FORGIVENESS AND
RE-EMPOWERMENT AFTER SEXUAL TRAUMA

Table of contents

Acknowledgments

A book is never the result of just the author, there are always others behind the book and behind the author that made it possible.

First and foremost, I thank the Warriors and the Redeemed Soul who are the book and without them the book would not be. Their openness, rawness and just their willingness to share their story in the hope it helps someone else is nothing short of divine.

Thank you to my family and thank you to my friends who are always fascinated and supportive of what I do regardless if I am going through an up or down.

Once again thanks to Karinya of PurQua Design Studio for another great cover design.

Thank you to Aussie star, author and advocate Sarah Monahan for writing the foreword, your time, consideration, words and support are highly appreciated.

Finally thank you to you the reader for the chance to help you in your time of need and during a very special part of your life's journey.

Sexual assault and childhood abuse can have a lifelong impact. They can shape the way we see the world and affect the way we live our life.

It can be highly traumatic, especially given the secrecy surrounding sexual trauma. It's not a polite subject to discuss, which not only stops victims from speaking up, but in many cases, it empowers the abusers to keep abusing.

It doesn't have to be this way. If as a society, we accept that sexual assault is something that happens to us, and just like if you were a victim of a natural disaster, a robbery, or a car accident, it's not our fault, and it's not something we need to keep bottled up inside. It happened to the victim. There's no need to feel shame, that it's just something that happened, like any other trauma, then victims wouldn't feel like victims forever.

Having gone through my own childhood abuse while working on the set of Hey Dad...! I understand what it's like to be hushed. I spoke up when it happened and was shut down. When I tried to bring it up again, I was again quietened. I knew what was happening was wrong, but that my safety was less important than the need for the show to go on. Thankfully, there were some people who also very quietly supported me and tried very hard to protect me. They kept me sane and gave me strength to not only stand up to Robert, but eventually quit the show.

When I finally went public; in a way I knew I couldn't be

quietened, it was terrifying, but also empowering. On one side many people tried to shut me down. Many called me names, I got threats, and I got people blaming me for what happened, but on the other side, I had thousands of people who contacted me to say thank you for speaking loud and proud. They had all too been victims of abuse, and they now felt empowered to also speak up. Most importantly, the police started an investigation, the other girls that Robert had abused also got to speak up again, and we sent a bad man to prison. One of the other girls told me that because of all us coming together, two legal precedents were changed in NSW law. The second precedent has changed how sex crime trials involving minors are conducted all over Australia. Generations of people will have access to justice that they would never have had, directly because of us.

The thing I learned most from the last few years, is that it's the stigma surrounding abuse that's the most traumatic. Yes, it's a horrible thing to happen, but we need to shift that horror to the perpetrator, and the act, and not to the victim. That old saying about a problem shared is a problem halved works just as well when it comes to sexual assault. If people can speak up freely about it, they can start to heal from it.

Now that it's not a dirty little secret, now that I don't have to pretend it didn't happen, now that I can speak loud and proud, I am able to live my life, and not be bound by my past. I'm free to move on, be strong, and even be an advocate for others.

I hope that everyone else who has experienced trauma can one day be like me, and all the brave souls in this book. I hope they can experience the relief of realizing that rape, assault and molestation doesn't have to define who you are. It can be something that happened to you, but it isn't all that you are.

Everyone in this book has a very different background, and different childhood. What they have in common is that a traumatic event happened to them. They all also learned how to cope. How to realize it didn't have to define them. It didn't have to roadblock them.

So many of us share this experience of abuse. If we could all stand up and share our stories like the people you're about to read about, I think we'd all be much better off.

So please, keep reading. Know that others have all been through a similar path, and they came out the other side just fine. You will too.

Sarah Monahan

www.sarahmonahan.com
Twitter: @Thesarahmonahan
Instagram: @Thesarahmonahan

GIFT 1: FREE FOR YOU ONLINE PROGRAM:

4 Fun Steps To Overcoming The Doldrums.

We all hit a plateau in our life, connect with your creative and authentic self and in 4 fun steps create, map out and action the next phase of your life. Be it a full major new chapter or just a minor direction adjustment.

Plus

GIFT 2: FREE ACCESS-MASIVELY IMPROVE YOUR MINDSET IN 30 DAYS:

30 Day Beat The Blues Challenge.

Do it on your own, with a friend or in a group, even at work. The 30 Day Beat The Blues Challenge is designed for you to take on simple but highly effective and specifically chosen tasks over a 30 day period. The sole purpose and aim of this challenge is to help you improve your mindset, for with an improved mindset comes improved outlook, improved decision making and therefore improved outcomes. You to can be manifesting greater results for you 30 days from now, start today.

Go to: www.yougotthismentalhealth.com.au/bonuses

GIFT 3: 2 COMPLIMENTARY TICKETS

Events by Petros (You Got This: Mental Health Services) are informative, empowering, practical and relevant.

You and a friend are invited to a non-workshop event and its Petros' shout.

With topics such as:

- Beating Panic Brain
- 3 Common things you do normally that you shouldn't do when having experienced a crisis or trauma
- 7 Steps to overcoming a crisis faster and better.

Use coupon code: RFTLBOOK on an eligible event you want to see. To be notified of upcoming events register through below link:

Go to: www.yougotthismentalhealth.com.au/events

*"All challenges, however heinous and difficult,
are across road where one determines whether
they become a victim or a victor"*

Petros 'The Human GPS' Galanoulis

INTRODUCTION

We are the smartest animals on the planet, we figured out the worst way to hurt each other giving us the title of the most brutal animals in the world. What sets rape and sexual assault above murder is, with murder you shoot or stab someone predominantly and they die, it is an awful thing, but it's done and dusted with. Rape and other sexual crimes penetrate much deeper, for they force a person to momentarily surrender their rights and access to their bodies and right to not be violated, their right to choose, they are hurt in the deepest most intimate way. Unlike murder it's not over, they don't die, at least not in the physical sense, instead they must live with it, bare a cross they did not deserve, nor ask for.

When I first had the idea about writing this book it was because I thought it would be a cool project to do, nothing more than that, there were the right intentions but it was just a project, until I sat for the first time to plan it and that raised a lot of questions for me and lead me to realise there were things I thought I knew but I didn't.

One thing that I came to realise is that often when these matters are reported they give the impression that once you become a victim, that's it you are a victim for life, your **diagnosis** is that in some way you are damaged or not going to be the same again. Although life certainly won't be the same, is the whole victim mentality true? Even necessary?

I continued with what was becoming a deep journey of discovery and self-realisation and a life lesson, I realised that the whole victim mentality was rife, the majority of the time that I saw a report or interview with a victim they always looked destroyed, understandable but what really stood out was that the victims all too often blamed themselves, this did not sound right, I couldn't help but ask why!?

Then things began to become even more interesting and curious and perhaps I was beginning to see one major issue when it came time to address the issues of rape and sexual assault, was this a gender issue...really?... or are we looking at this wrong?

I started to look in to incidents of rape of men, with all the male bashing aspect of this issue I was concerned the social attention was on the wrong spot or at least not wholly on the right spot, if we are to resolve this issue, we need to adjust our sight a little.

Up to 15% of men are raped or sexually assaulted, this however is an understatement as it is estimated up to 90% of rapes on males is not reported, the perpetrators are both women and men, with women more likely to perpetrate young children including their own, I also realised there is almost no services for male victims and the attitude was still very outdated and unsupportive of the notion men can be raped.[1]

I began to realise that this was not, in my opinion, a gender issue but a social issue, it was clear men were predominantly perpetrators in certain circumstances and in others were female. Gender should not matter, the fact that these acts happen at all should be the focus.

As I continued my research I realised most people were still a little uncomfortable talking about such matters, after all they are awkward and can be confronting; but it made me wonder whether perhaps there is not enough discussion going on in homes about these issues and at least what constitutes appropriate behaviour and how to develop healthy sexual and non-sexual relationships and conduct.

My final realisation was that there was some lacking in the books out there for recovering, not just dealing with but recovering from rape AND building a life that was better than it was even prior to the attack(s) primarily there was not much that was said from the perspective of both female and male victims and certainly I couldn't find anything that also gave the perspective of a rapist and with a specific angle.

So, what started off as a simple project developed, manifested in to a full-blown mission to bring to the world a piece of work that achieved several objectives:

Objective one- to show those struggling in the aftermath of a sexual infraction against them that it's not their fault, the idea of including an interview with a perpetrator is to add powerful proof that the victim is not to blame, as well as including the testimony of former victims who have positively transformed their lives who came to realise they were not to blame.

Objective two perhaps the most important one is that our life does not have to be over, you do not have to live a life of a victim and you can draw positives from your incident(s) and live a highly prosperous, abundant and happy life with intimacy included. Further this book aims to give those who have been raped or sexually assaulted an effective guide that has been

tried and tested over time and in some form by many other professionals and as guided by a group of people that have gone through it themselves,

Objective three to highlight that this is not a gender issue but a social one and man hating does not help. I found a mixture of female and male former victims for this very reason, to show that it can happen to either sex and to look at only who is doing to who mostly; is still leaving half the issue unattended and only half truths being put out in to society.

Objective four to encourage families to talk more at home about these issues and what constitutes healthy and appropriate behaviour and both relationship and sexual relationship development and attitude, **this work can also help a friend or loved one going through the tribulations of having been raped or sexually assaulted.**

These objectives are what my goals and aspirations are, that I hope to achieve by bringing this book to you, to the world, there will be plenty of insights and useable and effective information and access to professional help if you or someone you know needs it.

It would be remiss of me not to acknowledge the current wave of protest against sexual inappropriateness and this is excellent, it serves to outing incidences and giving victims some courage to speak, my angle is to show positive outcomes are possible and to show how they can be achieved.

There are several wonderful organisations doing great work however they can only do so much, not enough information available in the mainstream society for victims and minders or supporters of victims to use looking at this under-attended angle and media is more concerned with its own agenda which can skew realities.

My opening statement in this introduction is quite harsh and heavy but here is what I also know, I know that no greater and more capable and powerful animal or being than us humans exists on this planet for reducing and maybe one day completely eradicating incidents of rape and sexual abuse. We have the ability and means and the right spirit to achieve this, I hope that this

book can be for you and the world the match that lights the spark towards the achievement of this history making, world changing mission.

Furthermore I hope this book shows you that although your trauma may have snuffed out the light within you, it's not permanent, if you are thinking it's out permanently, not worth seeking for or you are seeking for the light within you once more but unsure, then let this book be your certainty that you can find yourself once more, an even better self as you are reaching for the light.

---

[1] NSW Health Education Centre, Against Violence, when a man is raped- A survival guide 2013

"When one finally truly commits to the first step; providence and momentum follow"

-Petros 'The Human GPS' Galanoulis

How this book works and its layout.

From this point on the contributors of this book when referred to collectively, are no longer referred to as 'victims' or 'former victims' or perpetrator or former perpetrator etc. as these are considered labels that perpetuate the negative psychology, instead they will be referred and appropriately so as 'Warriors'. The former perpetrator will be referred to as 'Redeemed Soul'.

Section one will consist of a set of 16 specific and laser focused questions that are posed to and answered by all the Warriors and the Redeemed Soul.

These questions are designed to take you the reader through their ordeal from a perspective that only those who have experienced such acts can know. This is to help understand a bit better what goes on from both the victim perspective and the perpetrator perspective

Out of that I hope to dispel any myths, develop new or different insights, perspectives and realisations and to educate society about rape and sexual assault and its truths. *Section two* I put together a 13-step healing process, this sequence is not the only possible sequence for healing, it's one I put together based on my years of both personal experience with another form of abuse and my professional experience with helping others deal with trauma or as I put it personal crises and grieving and healing from those. These are steps that the warriors could identify with therefore sharing how they did each step and their experience, my job in this section is to simply narrate and make it as simple and comfortable for these warriors to share their insight and advice.

This sequence is not a modality of healing such as CBT, Gestalt method or NLP it's a sequence of the stages of healing as I have come to know them and can be applied across traumas in general.

P.S. *Do enjoy the free gifts inside the book and the MEGA BONUS in the middle, also if you have the chance, check out our Facebook exclusive for readers and fans of the book and those who have their own similar story to share and or seeking answers, support , empowering-mind expanding life changing insights and guidance for tackling personal crises and trauma and developing greater resilience and coping skills for healing and thriving.*

Thank you and may you always live like you mean it.

"One is not defined by their falls nor their wounds or scars but their defiance, persistence, courage and fire to rise again despite the odds"

-Petros 'The Human GPS' Galanoulis

Who are the 'Warriors' and the Redeemed Soul'?

The Warriors and Redeemed Soul are at the surface a group of everyday folks from all walks of life like you and I who became extraordinary by way of an experience or set of experiences that many could not imagine going through. Yet these individuals took it on in a manner that makes them rather extraordinary and yet the epitome of human.

I include in this description the Redeemed Soul...... WHY?!!!...... I hear you cry, it's simple, this man perpetrated an awful act, this is undeniable however what he did afterwards and how he came together with his 'warrior' (all is revealed in the coming chapters) to redeem as much as one can, his actions are truly a show of understanding that what was done was wrong and that it created hurt and a broad spectrum of emotions and experiences. It shows remorse and a willingness to step up and take responsibility for his actions at the highest level and to use his unique and fascinating insight and perspective to positively help others where he possibly can, it is a great way to pay it forward and do some good.

He could have remained quiet, run from his act, continued down his dark path and completely be cold and indifferent towards what he did but instead he chose to face the toughest path......The path to redemption, forgiveness and healing in a time where someone who commits such an act may find it almost impossible to get those three things.

It is a testament to the character of all the Warriors for their contribution, it's not an easy thing to share necessarily but they as part of their journey have recognised the great good they can do by sharing their stories and letting you the reader in to a private and intimate part of their life in the hope that you or someone you know going through such a trauma may find healing, peace and forgiveness and go one to live not a normal life but an extraordinary life.

Sit back, relax and enjoy their story and the wisdom and guidance they provide and may you to live like you mean it from now and or once again.

The Warriors- Günther Frantz, Heather Morgan, Helena Nista, Kylie Bennett, John Elferink, Neil Whyte

Redeemed Soul- Gary (Book's name)

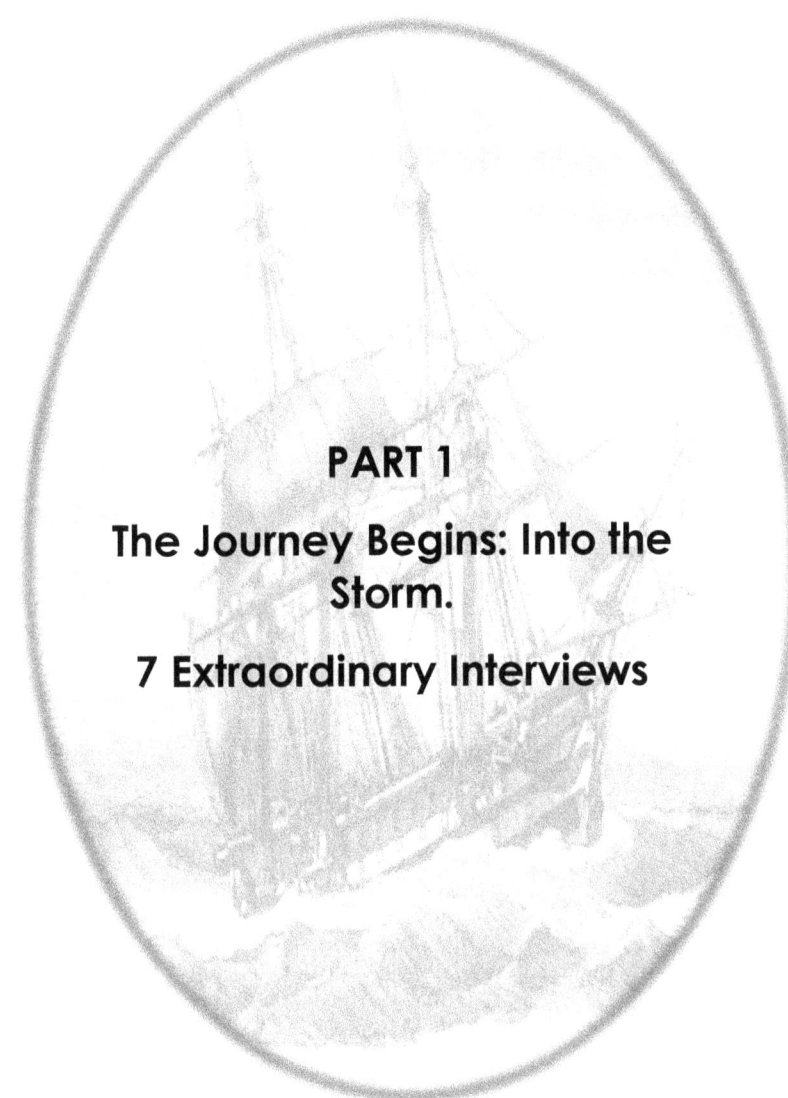

PART 1

The Journey Begins: Into the Storm.

7 Extraordinary Interviews

"Knowledge with action is power, it is the first step after deciding, for making great change of any size".

-Petros 'The Human GPS' Galanoulis

Petros' Thoughts.

From a young age I have had a strong curiosity and interest in the human journey and about why things are as they are and why people do what they do all the way to the deepest of questions like 'Who am I?', 'Why are we here?' Etc.

As I grew and learned and experienced more, which started early in life for me, from the age of nine I had to grow up, instead of being a typical child with a typical childhood, I began to see things, consistencies and anomalies both fair and unfair.

As I grew older one of those things was the issue of rape, molestation, sexual assault, I had a fascination behind the psychology and the creation of such desires within a person. I realised that through understanding why these acts occur will we have the best chance of reducing or dare I dream, completely stopping these acts from occurring. Eventually it also became a bit of a personal justice matter for me as a male.

I was fed up as a male being indirectly and maybe in some ways directly thought of as a sexual predator, a sleaze, a low level being that only thinks about sex and that's all he wants and that's the way to control me, that I'm not capable of much more than that, as someone who would unfairly and unjustly be potentially asked to sit elsewhere on a plane if a child sat next to me because I may be a sexual deviant all because I have a penis.

It seems I and many were being judged based on the behaviour of a minority and a misguided political ideology that says sexual crimes are a gender issue. I may sound extreme but if you stop and take a good look at it, I'm not that far off either and after all this is my thoughts not necessarily absolute social sentiment.

So, understanding that change begins with action and gathering facts, I found my 8 wonderful contributors and asked them some very specific questions allowing me to really get a true understanding, short of going through it myself, of what really happens when such an act occurs, what is truth and what is myth.

This is now what I present to you, thank you and enjoy.

Günther Frantz

Günther Frantz is a Public Keynote Speaker, Business and Personal Breakthrough Coach and Author who is based in Perth, Western Australia.

www.masteryourmindset.com.au

1.   What was life like before this happened?

My name is, Gunther Frantz, and I was born in Starnberg, Bavaria, to my beautiful parents Johann & Ingrid Frantz in April 1966. My father & mother have passed away in recent years. I am the fourth child with brothers and a sister still alive.

I would describe my childhood as a happy one. My father worked for the German Army and therefore, we lived in a small flat at the Army base in Feldafing where I shared a room with my two older brothers until I moved out at the age of eighteen. My father worked hard doing particularly long hours to make ends meet with my mother running the household.

As a child student I struggled a lot speaking and writing German. At the age of nine I was sent to a special German grammar class and repeated year four for failing to achieve acceptable marks. I was later diagnosed with dyslexia and my learning difficulties had effects on my social interaction with others. I was self-conscious, skinny and often bullied throughout my early school life.

During my childhood my parents were very supportive despite the fact my father was absent from the home for long periods due to his working commitments. Looking back, I became a 'mummy's boy' especially in the eyes of my brothers, who, whilst still enjoying a good relationship with me and my mother were far more confident and comfortable in social settings. My mother was a very religious woman with a strong Catholic upbringing in Bavaria. My father bordered on being an

Atheist. Dad would only go to church at Easter and Christmas, whereas my mother would have loved to go to church more often than the quite regular occasions that she did.

2.   Who were you before the attack?

Mum's input about God created a spiritual curiosity and interest in me from the age of nine or so. I went to the Catholic Church quite often by myself, either to the service on Sunday or Youth activities during the week. I didn't really 'find God' in the church and although I stopped going to church my spiritual hunger was still present. By the age of ten I developed a strong interest in swimming which soon occupied much of my time. I was introduced to swimming through my eldest brother, Phil who had belonged to the Starnberg Swimming Club for a couple of years.

My interest in swimming was the basis for positive change in my life. I developed a strong body and was acknowledged by the club for my high achievements. I would train at least six times a week and represented Germany on a National and International level from the age of twelve.

I believe things have really turned around for me from that point of time. I became a lot more self-confident at school and around my friends. My School marks improved, and I had many more friends with whom I enjoyed all the childish things one does at the age of twelve.

During that time my increased capacity for learning and applying the skills I had developed in my new-found identity (becoming a teenager), I felt a sense of responsibility to accomplish more complex tasks of which I was previously fearful of. Yet, looking for reassurance and acceptance became especially important to me at that time.

3. How did it happen, was it someone you knew and trusted or a stranger?

I met Scott Williams at the end of 1977 through my interest in swimming. I was eleven years old when I met him. He was a supervisor of the swimming pool in the German Army barracks. The swimming pool was made available to the public in the evenings and on the weekends. My brother, Phil, and some of our friends used the facility to train during the week. From there onwards I socially interacted with Scott Williams every second week in his employment capacity at the pool. I found him to be very friendly actively seeking me out to chat with.

Within about one year from knowing Scott Williams he was very comfortable around my friends and me.

He was very much the leader during any discussions as he was much older and presented as a leading figure on life and religion.

He presented as confident and knowledgeable. Around this time Scott Williams started to invite me and sometimes friends of mine to the sauna with him to discuss religious beliefs. I remember very early Scott Williams would tell us about social settings in European countries and Australia. He told us that many European countries and people seemed far more open about nakedness and it is usual practice for people to sauna and shower naked without any sexual leanings. At my young age I didn't really know either way. I hadn't experienced naked saunas or showers with other people, but I did not disbelieve Scott Williams.

The continued saunas and showers with Scott Williams continued from that point onwards whilst the religious discussion became deeper and intense. Scott Williams told me and others that he was appointed by the Lord proven by signs. He seemed to have a very strong understanding of the Bible. As I was young during this phase, between my twelfth and fourteenth birthdays I didn't think anything was untoward in the practice of showering and having saunas whilst naked with Scott Williams, who was an older man. Scott Williams had massaged me on occasions during these saunas, but they were what I believed to be sport massages focusing on my shoulders, neck, and on occasions towards my private parts which made me uncomfortable, but I thought it was not intentionally. Particularly with his strong Christian belief never did I suspect anything and at this time in my life I was totally naïve and had no sexual leanings, particularly not toward men, so I was never worried.

4.   Did you talk/ appeal to your attacker at the time?

Scott Williams increasing sexual advancement by massaging me all over my body when we were alone and touching my private parts intensified after my fourteenth birthday when I became a "born again Christian" and member of his church, Pentecostal Christian Church

At this point of time I looked up to Scott Williams as a friend and mentor. He was my spiritual guide. The significance of this occasion is from this point onwards Scott Williams became the highest authority in my life, not just in the spiritual sense but also as an adult from whom I sought guidance and instruction. I remember Scott Williams instructing me on this occasion on my path toward that rebirth as a true Christian. For two years I had already been receiving biblical instruction and training for between five to ten hours per week and when Scott Williams was not at the swimming pool he would give me religious material to study.

From this point forward, Scott Williams taught me and expected me, to massage him nakedly from top to bottom, front and back. Scott Williams exposed his genitals and encouraged me from the age of thirteen to touch him. I remember feeling very uncomfortable and uncertain with the situation. At this time in my life I had no sexual experience and was very shy. I did question Scott Williams sexual behaviour towards me as I was brought up by my parents to believe that this was wrong between two men and biblically condemned.

Whilst I clearly told him on many occasions that I didn't want to touch his penis, that I didn't want him to touch my penis and anus and exhibited physical actions by crossing my legs and moving my torso to restrict or prevent him from touching my penis and testicles I couldn't prevent him from doing these things. I was indoctrinated and desensitised and believed his teachings. He was my Pastor, my guide and my life coach. He was instructing me on my path to be a better Christian and converting the masses. This is what drove my life.

5.   What was their response and attitude?

It became commonplace that Scott Williams would instruct me to massage him in the sauna mostly in the same room on those wooden slatted beds when we were alone together from the age of fourteen. He had massaged me regularly citing the need for such remedial massage owing to my spiritual and church training. Right from the outset I felt uncomfortable with Scott Williams's insistence that, 1) I disrobe and be naked with him and 2) that he massaged me, and I massaged him all over the body, top to bottom, front and back, between the legs and seeing his penis exposed.

When I questioned this behaviour, Scott Williams stated that there is nothing wrong with touching a male body – it is Scriptural like Jesus and John or David and Jonathan in the Bible. I did not question the doctrines interpreted to me at that time. Notwithstanding my reluctance I never felt that I could go against his demands of me which increased each month. I saw him as the highest authority on earth, even at this early stage, I was honoured to be in his company owing to his spiritual and Christian standing.

Scott Williams commenced and continued with biblical phrases to justify his behaviours toward me. He always said, "how can I use you in the work of the Lord if you do not show love, God has brought you to me. I must instruct you in your walk and God demands complete surrender of body, mind and soul." There were so many phrases which were either directly from the Bible or interpretations (now I know they were incorrectly interpreted).

Scott Williams twisted Biblical Doctrine of male friendship, especially that of David and Jonathan in 1 Samuel 18, or Christ and his Apostles, in particular the preaching associated with 'Bundling' (Bundschaft- means a covenant friendship) and the need for a close relationship between men.

The total control Scott Williams had over me from an early age was the fact that I complied with every demand that he made of me. I dearly wanted to earn his favour owing to my belief that through him I would see my own salvation into the Kingdom of God.

6.   What's going through your head during the attack?

I was still a virgin, heterosexual and very confused by the actions of the man that I respected most on this earth. He was my religious Leader and life mentor owing to my strong faith.

I was basically desensitised and somewhat brainwashed as I never had any homosexual tendencies, but I was so entrenched in the teachings and power of Scott Williams that I allowed those sickening things to occur. They intensified very quickly, and Scott Williams's sexual action did not just involve having naked massages or touching genitals, but I will spare you the details.

He clearly knew that I wanted no part of it and didn't want to do it but his continual preaching and power over me enabled him to control my behaviours for his own depravity. I remember that I was petrified, shaking and very scared, yet I kept on going back to the pool, I didn't tell anyone, I don't know why, don't ask me as I don't know.

Unfortunately, I didn't tell any one of those 'attacks' and they continued for over 20 years of my life. The manipulation was based upon a lot of emotions. It sickened me. All I wished for in my life was that it would stop!

7. It finally ends, what are you thinking at that point and what do you do next?

For months, more like years Scott Williams would constantly tell me that; "you must surrender your mind, body and soul to me so that you can be trained. How can I use you in the work of the Lord, how can I give you the knowledge if you will not surrender to me?"

Statements such as this were quite often punctuated with harsh and threatening phrases such as "you heathen dog, surrender or you will never enter the Kingdom of Heaven, I must instruct you." The punishment for non-compliance was the highest punishment imaginable in both the physical, emotional and faith sense. One (1) you would be banished from the church and two (2) you would not enter the Kingdom of Heaven.

To a person of my faith the consequences of non-compliance, even the physical and emotive force, from Scott Williams who held the most powerful position in my life was not bearable. I was not armed with the physical, emotional and educational strength in these early years to deny Scott Williams, as will be evident by later accounts it took me the larger part of my life to have the emotional strength to leave Pentecostal Christian Church and my perpetrator Scott Williams.

8. Did you tell anyone: If Yes, who and why and how did they react? If No, why? How long before you did tell someone and why?

The other highly significant point of this experience was Scott Williams's insistence that I not tell any of my religious or social contact with him to my parents. That was not to say that I couldn't mention my friendship with him, but he was insistent that I not mention anything about what occurred in the swimming centre to my parents. He told me that I could not tell my parents about the naked saunas, naked showers and the religious instruction. He said that I was not yet trained and didn't possess the tools to convert my parents to a true Christian life. Without the training and guidance, I couldn't make them understand about the strong bond between men which I mentioned previously. Looking back, I am certain that this was another stage in the grooming process of Scott Williams toward me.

It was during the summer of 2006 that a church member approached me with a concern that one of my nephews was sexually abused by Scott Williams. I guess this was the icing on the cake. Another family member destroyed by Scott Williams. During those years leading up to that moment I had a lot of long conversations of the spiritual, financial, emotional abuse from Scott Williams and the PCC (Pentecostal Christian Church) with a couple of close friends. This was the first time in my life where I shared my story of sexual abuse with my two friends. Both were shocked, yet not surprised…

So, hearing about my nephew's experience and getting it confirmed by himself I and two church members decided to write a letter to Scott Williams and I added the last paragraph of the 11-page letter next:

(Private letter to Scott Williams – 7th September – 2006)

Private issue of Scott Williams making "sexual" advances on men

The reason why we put this paragraph at the end is due to its very delicate nature. We all had to "live with the consequences" for years each living in "almost denial and condemnation" not knowing that it also concerned many others.

No one of us was game to talk about the issue at stake and it took a lot of overcoming and finally opening up to be able to talk about personal experiences. This was also triggered by other members who have approached us for counselling regarding this issue.

We have now found out the very opposite is the case.

Those concerned have privately confessed to us seeking for counsel.

Scott Williams you know yourself that you have made sexual advances on too many men over too many years.

A "one off slip" could easily be excused and brought under the blood, but this is not the case – it is an ongoing problem and we feel it is our duty to protect future "victims" as much as yourself as you seem not have been able (or willing) to overcome this sin.

You easily send others onto a guilt trip of holding up the work of the Lord due to not having overcome sin, and yet you yourself are seemingly not willing to change and overcome. We are worried about your salvation. Similar to the fact that you do not want to hear that you should take it easier in working on the computer or being involved in the assembly…. The stroke you suffered last year has been brought on partly by yourself and we believe the Lord wanted to show you something to learn from and repent of. Please do not take these lines lightly as they are written after months of thought and prayer and with a heavy heart that things get worse in the assembly instead of better.

All the worse the individuals concerned were "pushed" into these situations under the "guise of surrendering". This guilt has caused them to live in hiding and condemnation. There are those who have lost their faith in the process, due to these situations.

Where has the church been to "uphold them with the truth"?

This must be put to an end and the scriptures demand reconciliation.

"The truth shall set you free"

We arranged a meeting to discuss with Scott Williams the letter and in his usual manner, he explained everything away, questioning our loyalty to his office and church. Even when he came to the last point about the sexual abuse he looked at me and stated that it only happened a few times. At this moment I boiled over, told everyone the truth that it happened hundreds of times to me over all those years and what a liar he is. I stood up and had to calm down before joining them again a few minutes later.

I reported my abuse to the NSW Police in Coffs Harbour at the end of 2006. I signed my final NSW Police Witness Statement of 88 pages on July 24th, 2010.

9. How did you initially deal with what happened to you?

I believe the degree of trauma associated with abuse will be related to many factors, including the relationship with the perpetrator, the severity of violation, the use of violence, age of perpetrate and/or victim, and duration of abuse. However, in every case of sexual abuse, the life of the individual has been damaged and violated. And dealing with it once I was 'free' of the long-term bondage was rather scary.

I encountered lack of self-esteem. I battled with low self-esteem, including self-hatred, suicidal depression and a sense of hopelessness.

I felt guilty. I battled with feeling guilty because I believed that I in some way was responsible for the abuse occurring.

I bottled up anger. I battled with not giving myself permission to be angry with the perpetrator and by misdirecting it, my most loved ones were caught in the line of fire.

I had post-traumatic stress. When neither resistance nor escape is possible, I felt my self-defense was non-existing due to its long-term occurrence.

I find it hard to trust. It is easier to cope with hate than with potential danger of love.

I felt shame. It condemned me for who I really am. I have a deep sense of grief. I grieve over what is lost and can never be replaced.

I lived in denial. I tried to deny the abuse, mislabeled it and minimised the damage. I knew I needed help. Though confused in many ways of what really had happened in my life I started to search for answers to all those strange feelings I suddenly encountered.

10. Did you blame yourself and if yes why and how did you realise it wasn't your fault?

I blamed myself because I let the abuse go on for so long. I felt it was my fault because I didn't tell anyone. I feared not being obedient to God and understand His Will communicated by Scott Williams. I was afraid of punishment, of being excommunicated by the church and that no one would believe my story. Looking back as an adult at the reasons I had for not telling makes me feel like, "I was so stupid to believe that threat".

Blaming myself was another technique to survive. It was an attempt to take control of a terrible situation where actually I had no control at all. To some extent I tried to change the past through self-blame, but as long as I did that, I remained a victim to the past. Once I acknowledged that it wasn't my fault, I was released from blame and started to be empowered. I became aware that I can't change the past, but I am able to be healed by letting go of blame and guilt.

After many years of personal self-development, research and speaking to other survivors I have learnt that it wasn't my fault. I learnt that self-blame is something which is very important to overcome because it can serve as a barrier to my healing process for the reason that it results in avoidance of reality. Once I understood the reality that my abuse was the fault of the perpetrator who abused me, and that the responsibility lies with them entirely I was free of self-blame.

11. What was the defining moment where you decided you would fight for and regain your life?

* I have answered this question in Q 8

12. How do you look at the attack now? Have you forgiven-Why or why not?

I started to share my story when I was in my early forties. I was sexually abused by the self-appointed founder & pastor of the church, Pentecostal Christian Church Due to my religious environment the common response I got from church members was "Have you forgiven him?" At that point of time I was afraid not to forgive, because of the churches reaction or being a bigger sinner…

The abuse kept me living in fear and on top of the list of fears was the fear of abandonment. So, what would happen if I didn't forgive? Would I find only disapproval and rejection by my Christian friends, my family and more importantly, by God? Unless I was prepared to spend eternity apart from God's presence, I had to forgive. I was taught that un-forgiveness was, after all, far worse than anything that was done to me. It seems that to refuse to forgive made me worse than the abuser, especially due to his standing within the church.

But the secret of forgiveness, regardless of whether I wanted to use it as a method of detachment or a way to move forward, is to focus, not on the abuse, but on freeing myself of the emotional pain I experienced as a result of that abuse. Once I made that decision, I felt lighter, freer and happier than ever before. I understood that I was victimised, but I am not a victim.

Forgiveness has empowered me to take control of my emotional wellbeing.

13. What was your position on sex after the act and what is it today, did you lose your liking etc. for sex or did it come back etc.?

Given that the sexual abuse involved unwanted sexual contact and inappropriate exposure over such a long time, I found myself very confused during those years regarding sexuality. Lots of difficulties appeared during my twenty-four years of marriage and it felt like being an emotional Yo-yo. Sex within the context of a loving relationship was probably greatly impacted by the following feelings I encountered.

- I had experienced difficulties in achieving sexual arousal or ejaculation.
- I felt distressed, shameful and guilty about certain sexual responses, interest or fantasy.
- I was feeling increased confusion during sexual and emotional intimacy.
- I was taught limited types of sexual activity were considered okay or enjoyable and others were forbidden.
- I disengaged emotionally due to flashbacks during sexual activity.
- I felt discomfort with being touched in certain areas of my body.

During and after my marriage break up I decided to receive help from trained professional therapists. It really helped me to have guidance and support during those difficult times. I discovered that I often found myself "somewhere else" mentally when the abuse happened.

Unfortunately, I carried this disconnection into my marriage relationship and it had a huge impact on my sexuality. Though, once I understood what I needed to work on, I wanted to learn to love my body and started to believe that I deserved to have a good sex life. I kept on thinking about the kind of relationship I wanted to have and regain control of my sex life. In the last seven years I have moved towards healthy sexual attitudes and reactions with my beautiful partner. The passing of time and positive sexual experience with my partner has naturally moved me towards a healthier sexual attitude which I am thankful for.

14.   Are there any positives from your situation?

It taught me self-awareness which gave a clearer perception of my own personality, including my strengths, weaknesses, beliefs, thoughts and emotions. As I developed my self-awareness I was able to make positive changes in my thought patterns.

Changing my interpretations of issues in my mind allowed me to change my emotions which gave me the ability to create what I wanted. I have now learned to focus my attention, emotions, reactions and behaviour in mastering my life.

Having self-awareness allows me to take control of my

emotions and I can make the desired changes I want, at the same time it permits me to understand other people better.

I have learned to accept responsibility. Even though I know it was not my fault, it is my responsibility to begin to develop necessary health-coping skills that will give me wanted results for my life. Nobody else will do it for me, it is up to me to make the changes. I can't change the past and I am not in control of circumstances, but I am always in control and responsible for my attitude and reactions. It is so easy to search for a scapegoat when things go wrong in life, we look to blame somebody so that we do not have to accept responsibility for our outcomes - but I found this approach very harmful and toxic to adopt. I became solution-focused which created in me the power to learn new skills. I live by the motto "stop learning, stop growing" which I believe is the key to growth and developing positive coping strategies.

15. How is life now compared to before the attack?

Let's face it, everyone hopes they'll avoid the worst life has to offer; accidents, illness, loss or violence etc. Unfortunately, few of us will get through life unscathed and the earlier we realise that we are not the only ones who have suffered the sooner we will be able to move on from our traumatic past.

Emerging on the other side of the pain, I now feel a much greater inner strength and have re-oriented my live towards more fulfilling goals. The suffering that resulted from those horrible experiences was not an endpoint. Instead it acted more as a catalyst to change for the better in all aspects of life. Probably it has sent me on a quest I would never have found otherwise.

Given the right mindset and environment I was able to reflect on the trauma, the suffering and struggle as an opportunity to search for meaning in my life. Ultimately to become a better version of myself because growth begins with healing from the suffering experienced.

I love this quote by Steve Maraboli "You are not a victim. Your story isn't over. No matter what you have been through, you're still here. Everyone who ever bet against you was wrong. You have a history of victory." I do feel I go from victory to victory even though sometimes success doesn't come easy, but I refuse to give up until I reach my goal.

A life of regret is no life at all and I can honestly say I do not have any regrets in my life. Sure, we all have regrets for things we've done, mistakes made, and opportunities lost. But I make a conscious decision every day of my life to minimise those moments of remorsefulness and lead a happier more fulfilling life than ever.

16.   Who are you today?

If you were in my head during the first few years I struggled after my trauma, you would have heard definitions that sounded like, "I am no good. I am useless. I am at fault. I am crazy. I am an idiot. I don't know who I am." The terrifying thing was, I believed it. Those statements weren't a true description of who I was, but I believed it.

The day I began to redefine myself in ways that were meaningful and positive I created a new self-definition. I will never be who I once was because of what I have been through. I am not who I was thirty, ten, or one year ago. Today I don't worry what people think of me. I allow myself to be who I am - the real me. Therefore, I want to turn trauma into purpose and use it to help others.

Through personal development courses over the last decade, I have been able to change my world around. I am a sexual abuse survivor. I can tell you what the abuse felt like for me and what kind of healing process got me to where I am today. Therefore, my goal is to spread awareness of the nightmares of victims of sexual abuse encounter.

I have dedicated my life to seeking remedy and resolve for victims of child sexual abuse. My story represents hope for the hopeless.

I want to help others see that it is worthwhile to tell their story and pursue liberty and freedom with the knowledge a person should never feel shame or guilt because of others' wrongdoing.

In the last years I have run my own business (Master Your Mindset & Relationship) which helps people to live their life successfully through a better understanding, whilst providing techniques to reach their unique strengths, abilities, passion, and values. I believe that wellness starts from within and everyone has the ability to become who they are. You deserve it, and you know you do, we all do.

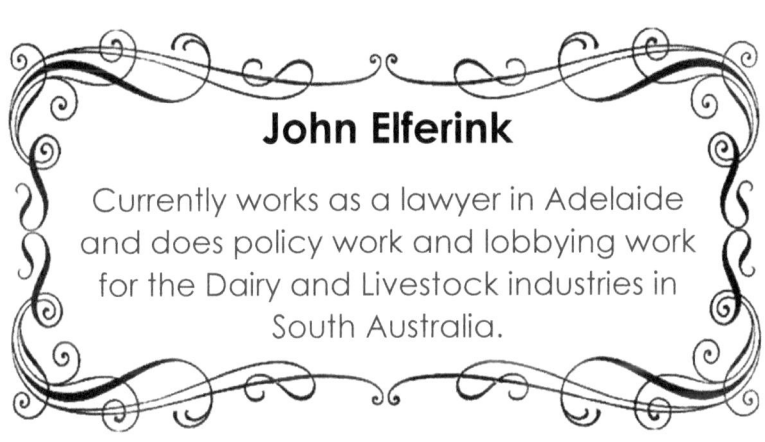

John Elferink

Currently works as a lawyer in Adelaide and does policy work and lobbying work for the Dairy and Livestock industries in South Australia.

1.   What was life like before this happened?

To give context to my life prior to the sexual assaults it is necessary to wind the clock back to the second world war. I was born in 1965 but both of my parents were profoundly affected by that dreadful calamity. My mother who was a little girl, having been born in 1937, was interned in a concentration camp with her brother and sister. The camp was governed by the Japanese on the island of Java which is now part of modern-day Indonesia.

The camp reserved for women and their children was an exercise in barbarism and awfulness. She lived in that camp for over three years and during that time she contracted illnesses that saw her circumstances declared to be hopeless and terminal. My mother's brother did not survive the camp and died in circumstances that were so spiritually crushing for my grandmother that I do not believe that she ever truly recovered from them.

My father on the other hand lived in Nazi occupied Holland. Suffering privations during that time was a matter of course for the Dutch and on his 18th birthday the German Government of Holland visited my father's home where he was taken off for forced labour in February 1944. Fortunately for my father he was able to escape his circumstances in June 1944 on D Day.

The Germans were distracted on that day for some reason.

After the war both my parents showed all the signs of the listlessness of their generation. Both could not bring themselves to stay in Holland, where my mother had returned to after the defeat of the Japanese. My father had three children by his first wife but that was a marriage doomed to fail. Dad couldn't get out of Europe quickly enough. Europe after the Second World War was not only financially bankrupt but spiritually as well. German post war literature reflected a ghastly exhausting nihilism. Books like the Clown by Heinrich Boll stand as monuments to that wreckage. Equally the victor's literature Orwell's 1984 also reflected the paucity of optimism that pervaded that battered part of the world.

My parents met in Ankara, the capital city of Turkey. They were married in Istanbul soon after and they continued to drift around the African coast of the Mediterranean returning periodically to Holland to birth children in their home country. As my mother relates the story I was conceived in Benghazi in Libya and born in Holland. That listlessness was what finally saw my parents cast an eye in the direction of Australia. While intending to land in Melbourne my father discovered Darwin and my mum dutifully came along. The simplicity of Darwin in the late 60s with its absence of television, tropical weather and swaying palm trees was enough to contain the wander lust that my parents had so long been infected with.

This wonderfully exotic and still far flung corner of the world was where I grew up in a household with substantial unrequited issues. My father's drinking certainly was a source of strain in the home but my mother's neurosis about his drinking reflected her insecurities as well.

The home was certainly not abusive, but both my parents were involved with their own internal dilemmas. We were not a family that appeared dysfunctional from the outside and even internally on the scale of dysfunction we were certainly no worse than many other families even in Darwin at the time.

Nevertheless, from my earliest memories I recall that my predominant emotions were fear and insecurity. I found it difficult to connect with my parents as my father had become increasingly remote as his drinking became more regular and the tension in the house increased. My relationship with my mother had been reduced to me silently sitting in the lounge room at home looking at the cover of a Mills and Boons romantic novel which had become the castle in which my mother took succor. At one point she had literally hundreds of those books in her bedroom cupboard.

So, by the age of 12 the answer had become attention seeking behaviour which became manifest by 13 in a series of petty crimes committed in the neighbourhood including a number of house break ins in local homes.

Naturally, it wasn't long before I was caught. My parents paid back the money that I had stolen and then they decided to make me pay them back by taking a job at a local nursery run by a family friend, Denis Arthur Hearne.

2. Who were you before the attack?

Lacking in confidence, inclined to self-pity and fearful. These are these are the emotions that I primarily remember of my childhood. That is not to say that there weren't moments of fun or joy, there were, swimming in my local creek was a great pleasure to me particularly when I was alone. In the tropics the dappled sun filtering through the leaves of tropical trees was the water babbled over nearby rocks provides a very peaceful frame of mind. Whenever others were around I often felt a resentment to their presence.

Dealing with other kids was always something that I didn't do well. Truth be known I still don't make friends easily. I couldn't help being possessed of a nagging feeling that there was a secret in the world that would give you entry to that world with friendships and connection with others but for some reason that secret was being kept from me. That awkward sense of isolation would visit me often and cause me to try far too hard to belong. That world view made me extremely vulnerable to suggestion and left me with few hand brakes or filters to stop me.

3. How did it happen, was it someone you knew and trusted or a stranger?

The platform to the exposure has already been outlined. I needed a job to pay back money that I had stolen. The job was a weekend job paid at $2 per hour to pay back the money. As the perpetrator already was a family friend he offered the work and I was then set to work in Tropicus Nursery in Darwin.

It wasn't long after that the perpetrator set about seducing me. (That was how he saw it), it was rape.

4.   Did you talk/ appeal to your attacker at the time?

Not really. In an affectionless life any form of attention was attention. Having however said that I never enjoyed or sought out the experiences. But there were two forces at work, firstly, my fear of my enraged father who had made it clear to me that if I didn't make good on the money that I had stolen I was going to be in a mountain of strife and secondly, the rapes were not violent incidents in the first instances. Only with the passage of time did Hearne escalate his conduct to what was painful. By that stage his violations were of a most invasive sort.

The wrongness of it became more apparent over time. On one of the last occasions he took me to a local public toilet and invited the men there to join us in a change cubicle. There was a fellow who was having his liberty with me who whispered into my ear that he wanted me to come home with him. I responded to him that I couldn't because my parents expected me home soon as I has school the next day. When I said that out aloud it just didn't sound right, even to the ears of a confused boy. That was the last incident. I left his employ soon after because I had paid off the debt and I recall being happy to move on.

5.   What was their response and attitude?

His approach to his crimes was heavily loaded with self-justification. He would regularly pull me aside and explain to me the normalness of what he was doing with pseudoscience and social quasi-analysis. For example, he once told me that what was happening was normal as that there had been a study done in rat populations that were a population was too dense the male rats would begin instinctively to engage in homo-sexual behaviour to limit population growth and therefore what we were doing was merely a reflection of the increasing world population. Well that's alright then I suppose.

I have no doubt that he also saw himself as a guide. He found justification in is actions based on ancient Greek culture where such relationships were normal and therefore the sodomy of children was fine so long as it was done with the right intentions. In truth there was little in his conduct that reflected his assertions. When he wasn't raping me, or justifying his actions to me he was aloof, distant and dismissive. In short, he wasn't even living up to his own fantasy (More on that ahead).

6.   What's going through your head during the attack?

Get on with it. Pain did occur but more in the sense of a deep discomfort and therefore I just wanted it to pass. Compliance assisted that approach and therefore the act was over and done with normally within 20 minutes.

7.   It finally ends, what are you thinking at that point and what do you do next?

When I paid the debt, I bolted for the door, which took about 9 months. After that I soon secured other weekend work at a petrol station and later at Coles pushing trollies. I enjoyed the income and it went to support my growing drinking habit.

As time passed the square peg in a round hole became squarer and the feeling of loneliness and ongoing isolation became more pronounced. During the following years my resentments became deeper and I became exposed to a strong ever-present feeling of guilt and remorse.

My emotional states also tended to become more extreme swinging from pronounced lows to feverish highs.

8.   Did you tell anyone: If Yes, who and why and how did they react?

About 10 years later I told my first wife, as she was then, about it and she was horrified. I recall feeling a little surprised at her reaction, but she was also very anxious that I never raise the issue again in any circumstances with anyone. She never explained her response and I never enquired but in hindsight I suspect she just didn't know how to respond to such information so to not talk about it was the best option. I often think that the response by the Churches to their miscreant priests reflects an extension of that rationale.

9.   If No, why? How long before you did tell someone and why?

Except for my first wife I told no one. My life was already complicated, and liquor and the unhealthy pursuit of wanton women was now at the forefront of my mind. Acceptance by women in particular, was a central need and rejection by women was a central fear in my psyche. Rejection was a devastating blow each time that occurred. Most normal women had nearly every alarm bell ringing soon after talking to me, so rejection was common. Needy women, nevertheless, would be available and you don't have to be Dr Phil to appreciate how such relationships developed.

My silence of the years of even being a police officer was wrong. It is the only shame that I feel about the episode that it took me so long to report the matter. The only enfeebled explanation that I can offer for my silence was that I was still getting out of the mess that was my psyche and I didn't have the emotional capacity to deal with the matter in open court.

God or providence however forced my hand literally on the day that I entered my new parliamentary electorate office after I was elected. I had no staff the office was bare but for a telephone on the desk which was ringing. I answered the call, literally the first call that I ever took as a member of parliament, and it was a detective from Darwin doing an investigation into Hearn. My name had been mentioned as being distantly attached to Hearn's and she was just ringing to close off the lead.

So, there I was, would my first act as a member of parliament be to cover for the actions of a paedophile because it didn't suit me? I decided not. I called her back two days later with a fully crafted written statement and prepared myself to give evidence against him.

For his crimes against me he was sentenced to four and a half years of prison. He got out in two and one quarter.

10. How did you initially deal with what happened to you?

You get on with it. I wasn't talking to anyone. I wasn't working for him anymore and the debt had been paid.

I had developed a healthy appetite for liquor even before these events having experience alcohol for the first time at the age of five. I hated the taste but loved the effect. I was now seeking liquor wherever and whenever I could. Was it all linked? Probably, but the stealing, the love of being intoxicated, the exposure to the rapes were all, in my opinion, different facets and manifestations of the same flawed personality. (Don't take that to mean that I blame myself for the rapes. I just tried to use people and got used.)

11. Did you blame yourself and if yes why and how did you realise it wasn't your fault?

I don't think I sought to attach blame to it. I never felt guilty about those events per se. There was a much greater sense of guilt, remorse and fear that occupied my mind often not linked to any real events. If there was a link between the child sexual abuse and those emotions I never at the time, nor even today, make that link.

I suspect that my world view had become so corrupted that the boundaries between normality and depravity had become completely obscured. That's a dangerous place to be because nothing in such a paradigm is real. For those of us who have experience an earthquake the sensation is awful not because it hurts but because what we know to be true, i.e. that we can stand on the ground, isn't true anymore. There is no truth. This is nothing solid, stable or dependable. All is confusion, and all is uncertain. Make the earthquake last years, instead of minutes and that was my state of mind. No moral standard was stable, no emotion was dependable, no relationship could stand on the liquefaction that served as my foundations.

12. What was the defining moment where you decided you would fight for and regain your life?

29th of September 1986 I fell off the cooling pipes that ran the air-conditioning system in the Darwin Casino. I drunk, confused and I don't doubt that I was presenting as someone who had a mental disorder. I presented in such a wretched state no charges were proffered, and I was merely taken home. My world was shattered. I had come to a crisis and I knew that I was going mad. My drinking was raging out of control to match the human who was raging out of control. My fears and resentments had become so strong that I felt they were about to suffocate me. I had collapsed into a hole that I thought there would be no return from.

I would have been happy to die and often thought about the blessing that the oblivion of death would be. Perchance to dream, was enough to make a coward of me.

13. How do you look at the attack now? Have you forgiven-Why or why not?

Indifference. 40 years of life has passed and too many

slings and arrows have faced to have any lasting impact. 31 of those forty years have been alcohol and drug free which has done much to restore stability to my existence. That does not mean that I am absolved from pain or suffering it just means that I can pass through my world in peace.

As for Hearn. If I have any emotion toward him today it is irritation. Not necessarily because of what he did to me but because of what he wasted. He was, (I suppose still is), a smart man with a good business and a prospective future. He chucked it all out of the window to pursue raping boys. (He was eventually convicted of multiple crimes).

There is no forgiveness from my perspective, what happened, there is little to add to that. I have never asked him to apologise and he has never offered. I couldn't care if he did. I am not going to hand over my happiness to a paedophile and wait for his apology.

If I cannot form my own happiness without his contrition, then I have still left him in charge of my emotional state. To hell with that.

However, there was one time that an emotion surfaced that shocked me. I had children and when I was about 40 I was with my infant daughters at a public place in Darwin. Hearn had been released from prison for some time. He walked around the corner at that place and he looked at me and then down at my infant children.

Something very deep and very dark stirred into life in me and it came from the very deepest reaches of my lizard brain. I didn't move but something must have been telegraphed because he immediately scurried off as quickly as he could, and I felt my wife's hand take my arm. Had he smiled, or in any way motioned to my children I am certain on that occasion that there would have been a homicide.

Whilst my wife had never seen or met Hearn she knew exactly who he was because of the change in my demeanor. I suspect it was merely a protective instinct that has evolved into the human psyche over millennia to protect one's young. But if it was then it is a force that is much deeper and dangerous than I have ever imagined up until that time.

14. What was your position on sex after the act and what is it today, did you lose your liking for sex or did it come back etc?

Sex was never a problem, but homosexual acts hold no interest to me whatsoever. I have no issues with those who engage in such practices by I am possessed of no inkling in the least form to ever experiment or engage in such conduct with another male.

Sex to me has become much more about the intimacy and connection one can have with another. It's not a tool of conquest but rather a shared experience of intimacy. One of the great things that I read about sex; years ago, was the notion that the Ancient Greeks had some six words for love.

Two of them stood out and I wish my attacker, who so loved to use ancient Greek culture to justify his crimes, took the time to understand what the Greeks were banging on about. I just want to focus on two words they used, "Eros", and "pragma".

Eros is self-explanatory, and we see it everywhere. It was the superficial, and potentially harmful pursuit of one's own lustful desires. It is essentially only about the person

who feels it and while it may be fun between two who experience it, it is about taking not giving it is about what you can get out of the act. It was considered dangerous by the Greeks.

Pragma is the one I aspire to. Picture this if you will, your wife, (husband) of 30 years gets out of bed one morning and her breath smells like it could strip paint of the side of a battleship. She scratches her bum and the elastic has given way on one side, so her knickers are creeping up her bum crack. As she walks across the bedroom the filtering sunlight from the window catches her cellulite in a most unflattering way.............and all you can feel is overwhelming love and you nearly weep with gratitude for this vision of companionship that is manifest before you. That's pragma. Boom.

15. Are there any positives from your situation?

Many I would suggest. In the years that followed that calamitous evening at the Darwin Casino I launched into getting better. I read veraciously, nothing was of the table, self-help books, religious works, philosophical works. Every idea was listened to many discarded but as many retained.

What happened was a wonderful, scary and what seemed insurmountable journey. Often frustrated, but also rewarded. After a year of trying to get better I was at a meeting where I was feeling resentful and despondent that my depressions, resentments and guilts were not seeming to abate. As usual I was drumming my fingers impatiently on the table in front of me brooding on the wretchedness of my life. (Self-pity was a strong suit for me). As my fingers drummed on the table I became aware of the sharp report of fingernails on the table top.

I turned my hand over and looked at my fingernails and noticed they needed to be trimmed. Up until that time I had never in my life needed to trim my nails, because I chewed them. I chewed them often until they bled. Yet here was evidence that something had changed. This may sound odd, but I was astonished. Despite my best efforts to wallow snout deep in self-pity my inner being was showing signs of increasing peace. That growing was becoming manifest in a small way with my unmolested fingernails being pointers. I still recall going to a chemist to buy my first set of nail clippers ever. The sensation was the same sensation I got many years later when I was presented my first degree.

16. How is life now compared to before the attack?

That I cannot compare. The life of a child is different to the life of an adult. What I do know is that with the passage of time since my early 20s I have come to know serenity. (Albeit occasionally).

17.   Who are you today?

In short, I am a participant in the world. I have come to dislike the word "survivor" when referring to my child sexual abuse. A survivor of a shipwreck is the baffled soul sitting on a beach after being washed ashore. They're confused about the trauma they've endured, and they look back to the sea that washed them onto that beach as they contemplate how it could have been. I left that beach decades ago. Survive, nuts, I have gone to thrive. That is not to say it hasn't been without challenges. I once had a Minister of the Crown call me a "poofter" in parliament as he reflected on that abuse.

Unkindness will always be there in the hearts of others. For them I feel compassion and hope that they will become more noble with the passage of time.

From being a petty housebreaker, to paedophile's target, to alcoholic, to policeman, Member of Parliament and Minister of the Crown including and Attorney General the journey has been surprising. But at least I haven't been bored.

Kylie Bennett

Kylie Bennett Works as an emergency communications officer; answering 000 calls, dispatching resources and monitoring radio channels. Kylie also owns a pet minding business offering pet minding and wedding assistance, so couples can have their fur-babies at their wedding Australia wide.

Kylie is based in Queensland
www.petweddingservices.co

1. What was life like before this happened?

My childhood was one of happiness; I went to a good school, grew up on the Gold Coast but in a rural area, had every pet any animal loving girl could want. Both my parents were supportive and loving, worked hard to let my sister and I have what we had. I knew who I was and what I wanted to achieve, I was great at school and loved my sports. Hated Brussel-sprouts, still do. Leading closer to the incident my life was pretty good, I had just gotten everything back on track after breaking up with my boyfriend (the attacker) that I had left my home town (I moved to Toowoomba and two weeks in he broke up with me) to be with and moved back to the Gold Coast. I was fortunate to be settling back into my old job and had a great place I was renting.

2. Who were you before the attack?

I was me, I was whole, I was the bubbly girl who had no problems in the world and everything going for her. I was confident, ambitious, driven, happy, outgoing and full of life, gave everyone the benefit of the doubt, trusted instantly. But most of all I was just simply me. It's hard to describe the person you are in words, without ever meeting that person face to face but I am sure we all know someone similar to who I was then.

I got this from a friend after the attack, it was their thoughts when they first met me.

"She was beautiful and radiant, she stood out from the crowd. She put a smile on people's faces, she was amazing and centered and she was so intriguing, and she was so bright and bubbly."

3. How did it happen, was it someone you knew and trusted or a stranger?

It was my ex-boyfriend, we had dated a short amount of time before breaking up – 4 months. We had a planned a holiday overseas together that he decided before we had broken up he no longer wanted to go on. There was about $1400 from his half that we couldn't get back and that I had paid so he agreed to pay me back by the end of 2015.

He sent me a text to say he had the money and wanted to end things on a positive note, so I agreed and after much back and forth of where to meet, we ended up agreeing on my place since he was from the country and wanted to see the beach while he was down my way.

This was December of 2015 and we broke up September 2015. He came down late one night during the week when I had mentioned that I was home alone. I never thought he was coming down to hurt me, I trusted him and while we were together there was never any real sign that he could be dangerous.

When he arrived, it was late about 11pm and I was already in bed, he was going to stay the night and we had discussed that nothing was going to be happening (call me crazy but I had no reason not to trust him). About 10mins after he got there he attacked, forcing me onto my stomach and beginning to try and zippy tie my hands behind my back, once I knew what was happening, I knew I was in trouble. I hid my left hand under myself and tucked in tight, he already had my left wrist in a zippy tie with my arm in a restraint hold, the kind police and bouncers use to get people to move on.

We struggled for a bit I wouldn't give him my left hand and each time I told him no he would pull my wrist further up my back causing more pain. I asked him why, what did he want, if it was about the money just leave and don't pay it back. But he wanted my phone pin, so he could delete all the messages to say he owed me the money and that he was going to pay it back and trying to black mail me. I told him my pin and my phone was within reach, but he wouldn't do it unless I was tied up. We struggled for about half an hour with immense pain in my shoulder and elbow. It was when he had me by the throat and threatened to rape me up the bum, that I gave up. I was not going to be raped if I could help it. I gave him my wrist and he zippy tied my hands behind my back. Once they were on he went through my phone and deleted everything, texts, photos, Facebook messages, his family. Everything. All while I was trying to get my hands free. Just as he said "Don't try you will never break them" at that very moment they broke. I am still not sure who was more surprised, him or myself. In that spilt moment there was a mini standoff, now what....?

I took off from my bed to the door, he blocked it and pushed me back onto the bed, so I tried again this time got a good kick to the stomach for my efforts. Well running was out. So I stood at the end of the bed with my hands up ready to fight (I had done a few years of boxing) He said "go on hit me, do it" I wanted to so bad, but it was almost like someone watching over tapped me on the shoulder and was like no, just talk him down, you can talk him down. Plus, my right arm was in no state to punch on, I could hardly lift it. And I knew it would be a punch on until someone was out cold. So, I talked to him, told him it was okay, that he had got what he wanted, he had scared me enough, and he could go now.

He wouldn't make eye contact just stared at the wall beside him. Finally, he came around and said he would go and would need one of the zippy ties still around my wrist. I tried to find a pair of scissors but of course they are MIA in the kitchen, then I handed him a knife, yes, I thought twice but I just wanted him out. As he placed the knife at my wrist blade side away from me he went to leverage the knife up. The tip of the blade dug into my arm and he stopped, looked me in the eye and said "I can't do that it will hurt you" I wanted to scream at him, what the Fuck was the last hour you Fuck-wit?!! But I stayed calm and got a pair of pliers (who has pliers in the kitchen and not scissors, turns out my flat mate) We cut off the tie and he went to the bathroom...... quick I thought you need proof.... So, I stashed a shirt he brought in his bag in my clothes basket and got my iPad and ran outside. I turned it on record and hid it in the garden. He noticed the shirt missing and found it whilst yelling at me from inside asking where I was and why. As he left he says "'I don't care how long I go away for, I will find you"-then smart arse me replied- "well the worlds a big place and I have a head start" As he drove off I tried to take a photo of his car, unfortunately he busted me and stopped. Got out of his car and went for me, I dodged and ran down the street to a neighbour's house while calling 000. He took ages to come down the street and when he did he was in his car.

He rang me from a private number, when I answered he told me he had stolen my cat and was going to throw her out the window on the highway if I called the police. I begged him to bring her back and that I wouldn't call the police. My neighbor came out to see if I was okay and he heard her talking to me, told me to tell her everything was alright. I did as I grab her arm, so she couldn't leave. Once off the phone I told her what had happened and asked her to be a witness to his car being here and to stay inside, she agreed (I was so lucky she worked in car sales so no mistake on the brand of car!) As he came back to give me the cat the police rang on a private number, thinking it was him calling me I answered, he saw me on the phone and took off with my cat. Once the police arrived they asked me questions, took photos of the scene and evidence. It's now 1am and I was taken to the station for a statement, 6 hours later I am released.

4.   Did you talk/ appeal to your attacker at the time?

I hadn't spoken to him since we had broken up apart from the quick text to remind him he needed to pay me back.

During the event I certainly tried pleading with him and talking him out of it, sometimes I was successful and others not so much so. During the actual attack where he was physically restraining me, I couldn't talk him down, I couldn't appeal to him, whimpering, crying, pleading, telling him I was scared and hurt didn't seem to make any difference. However, once I was free and able to fight if needed I could talk to him quite easily, it was like whatever was controlling him was gone and he could see some kind of reasoning. Either that or the reality of what he was doing hit him in that moment. I guess knowing what was going on in his head at the time will be one of my life's greatest mysteries.

5.   What was their response and attitude?

While he had me restrained no talking could possibly get him to see any sense- it was his way or more pain and fear. It wasn't until I got free that I could talk him down I was no longer directly under his power. It took some time, but I managed to get him to leave. During this period of talking to him he could hardly make eye contact with me, staring at the wall of my bedroom mostly.

6.   What's going through your head during the attack?

The moment I realized what was happening there was a sense of dread, fear, the moment that you think you're in trouble is something entirely different and so hard to explain. It's something that switches in you and you go from calmness thinking it's a bit of fun or a joke to the point of clarity, to pretty much that oh shit moment. I was so lucky that I had clear thinking, I remained fairly calm to my surprise.

To start with I wanted to fight and fight I did, I spoke to him, I yelled at him, I cried, I thrusted about, I offered what he wanted, but nothing was any good because at this point he didn't have what he wanted, my hands zippy tied behind my back. There was a struggle for some time, felt like forever as it does. I struggled for about 20mins or so and it was when he had me by the throat and said he would shove his cock up my ass that I gave in. I remember thinking I am not getting raped, I will sort out the zippy ties when they are on. Once the zippy ties were on I was thinking 'how can I get out of them'. Once they broke I didn't have a plan, and my escape was short lived. When he goes to the bathroom before he leaves, I think okay, proof now I need proof. I grab a shirt stuff it in my clothes basket and run to my iPad and set it on record and hide it out in the garden near his car, at least I can get his voice on there and I will have something to say he was here.

Okay, okay just breathe I thought he's nearly out of here. He jumps in his car and the last thing he says is "I don't care how long I go away for, I will find you" Brave me decided to spit back at him "well good luck, the worlds a big place and I have a head start" I don't even know where that came from. Then as he's driving out the drive way... my brain says proof... get more... so I take a photo of his car. Which of course he saw and stopped and got out... RUN, I legged it around him and down the street, hid in a neighbour's front yard and called the police. He was taking AGES to get back in his car and to leave, I'm thinking what are you doing? and then the phone call and my heart sank, and I felt like I was going to vomit. Nothing mattered now I needed to get my cat back...

I remember during the whole 6 hours with the police I kept saying just get my cat back. I knew he had drowned cats as a kid and I just couldn't bear to think about what could happen to her. When I was in the police car on the way to the station I remember saying to my angels, I'm okay, I'm okay now just look after my cat.

7. It finally ends, what are you thinking at that point and what do you do next?

Once everything was completed with the police they escorted me home and I went to work. I wasn't going to sit at home and freak out all day.

He proceeded to contact all my friends, even my ex - husband to get into contact with me after he was charged and released on bail. This was hard, now it's not just me involved. He even added me on snap chat with a fake name, flirted with me and even asked me out! It wasn't until his cousin informed me that it was him that I reported it to police.

The nightmares were hideous, trying to hide from him in a fully glass house while he tried to kill me was the worst one.

Did you tell anyone: If Yes, who and why and how did they react? If No, why? How long before you did tell someone and why?

When I got to work I broke down and started crying, said to one of the girls I worked with I just needed to quickly have a shower and I had had a long night. She said okay. Then I told the people I worked with and they were shocked and concerned, I did basic tasks throughout the day and the police called several times and popped into my work place as well. My mum rang the vet clinic late morning, close to lunch saying that a vet clinic in his home town had called and said my cat had been handed in.

Thank goodness. Mum asked why she was in

Toowoomba and I told her briefly what had happened. I quickly rang the vets and they reported that she was brought in soaking wet and I panicked requested they checked her lungs as he had drowned cats when he was younger, luckily it she was fine.

I told lots of people I wasn't going to hide what happened to me, if it could happen to me it could happen to anyone and talking about it was a way for me to cope to process it. Most people supported me so much and others couldn't handle my honesty and openness and I lost some friends for a little while in the process. But those handful of people that stuck by me held me together as best they could.

8. How did you initially deal with what happened to you?

I think I stayed in shock for a decent period of time, I put on a brave and strong face and did it well for a period of time. Fake it till you make it as they say. I spoke to family and friends, spoke with a counsellor, lived with a friend for the first few nights and then slept at home with all the outside lights on a knife under my bed. I would get anxiety seeing cars the same as his, finding myself checking number plates, or people that looked like him or wore the same cologne. I would often freak out late at night and head to a friend's house, taking my cat with me of course. She came to work with me every day for 2 months.

9. Did you blame yourself and if yes why and how did you realize it wasn't your fault?

No, I was lucky, I never blamed myself. I guess my situation is a little different since I didn't have much contact with him after we broke up. I did wonder why for a long time though.

10. What was the defining moment where you decided you would fight for and regain your life?

I was never going to let him beat me, but I struggled to regain my life for some time. I got to a point where I physically, mentally and emotionally had enough.

Physically

I had sustained an injury to my right shoulder and elbow, this affected every facet of my life. I was a veterinary nurse at the time, pet minder and dog walker, so my ability to work with animals was reduced dramatically. I was also at the time paid to ride horses, try doing that properly with one arm. I lived such a healthy and active life that this one injury also ceased my gym program and fitness competitions that I was entering at the time. Talk about effecting all your happy places and escapes! I now have a daily reminder in the way of the scar on my left wrist from the zippy ties.

Mentally

I suffered from anxiety, nightmares and paranoia after the incident. I would get anxiety when I saw a silver Hilux Ute, when I saw zippy ties (we use these at the vet clinic), number plates that held the same letters as his, places we visited together, being home alone - I ended up moving house, my phone ringing with a private number, seeing ADIDAS clothing or branding (he always wore this brand), I slept with a knife under my pillow, lights on in the house and outside, and even answered the door when I was home alone with 000 ready on the mobile and a knife in my hand. I had multiple nightmares of him trying to attack me and even kill me.

I second guessed some potential pet minding jobs, I was on edge and watching my back at shopping centers etc. There were nights that I was that scared that I left my home and stayed at a friend's house, putting my cat into work in the middle of the night, I took my cat everywhere with me for a short period after the incident. Sexually after the incident I could not share a bed with a man – one left in the middle of the night I was that anxious about falling asleep next to them. I would rarely have them at my house as I was not comfortable in not only them knowing where I live but also in my room.

Emotionally

I felt deflated and a shell of the person I was, I was on edge and uneasy, I was withdrawn, cautious, and scared of letting someone in again and falling in love, being vulnerable. I have always wanted to be a parent and after the incident I was petrified of the potential of bringing a little girl into a world that this could happen to her in. I had self-worth issues and confidence issues, I no longer trusted my sense of judgment and thought if I could be fooled by a boy like that then I couldn't trust myself or anyone else. I went to counselling. I was emotionally cold towards men. I used NLP process to help recover from the incident. Friends saw the difference in me, they said I wasn't the bright, bubbly person, I had lost my spark, I was jumpy, scared, defeated, and lost my smile. They were worried I wouldn't leave the dark place I had gone to and I was throwing myself into work even more than normal.

At this point I had to do something I knew I couldn't live my life this. So, I sought help through a friend that had done some mind work training called time line therapy. We completed this at the beginning of 2017 and I can now look back on what happened without feeling the anxiety, despair or fear that it caused, and it allowed me to open up and begin to become the person I was before. You simply cannot hold onto the hurt and pain forever, there comes a time you have to stop. I reached that moment, you will know it when you get there. It's scary and not easy facing it front on, but it is something that needs to be faced.

11. How do you look at the attack now? Have you forgiven-Why or why not?

I see it as a great learning curve not only for me but for him as well. I have forgiven him, I am so much stronger now than I was before, and I can see right through men. I am more appreciative in relationships as well. Forgiving him was something I never seconded guessed. I am not one to hold grudges normally and there had to be a bigger reason for him to do what he did. It was his issue not mine and I didn't need to carry the burden.

12. What was your position on sex after the act and what is it today, did you lose your liking for sex or did it come back etc?

I was nervous about being intimate again and certainly couldn't be on my back, held down or restrained at all. These things are slowing coming back and I am feeling more comfortable with it. But that is largely due to my current partner, who is so incredible about it all.

13. Are there any positives from your situation?

There are lots if you look.

- I am stronger

- I am more confident in myself as a woman, I survived that, that soul wrenching event.

- I can handle anything now. A guy plays me, see you later. Nothing is as hard as what I went through.

- I know who my friends are

- previously to this I had gotten through a divorce in 2013 so two major events in relationships and I am here standing strong and chasing my dreams.

He got help, he served time and he's moving on. Fingers crossed for his current girlfriend who a month after he got out of jail gave birth to their little girl.

14. How is life now compared to before the attack?

Life is pretty much back the same it was before. I am that person again but with the perks listed above. I will be honest I cannot take the full wrap for it. My friends, my family and my man have pulled me through. My current boyfriend went through hell to get a chance with me and the day we met was the first time in so many years that I felt like me, that I genuinely laughed and smiled and simply enjoyed life.

"You're not a victim for sharing your story. You are a survivor setting the world on fire with your truth. And you never know who needs your light, your warmth and raging courage" ~Alex Elle

15. Who are you today?

Today, I am me. I am working as a communications officer – the person you speak to when you call 000. I am also a successful business owner with a pet minding company expanding across Australia and recently purchased two competitors. I was a finalist at the young entrepreneur of the year awards for the Gold Coast in 2017 and 2018. I am ambitious, confident, happy and thankful. I am everything you read in the first paragraph but better.

And I hope you to will be the person you were before but more.

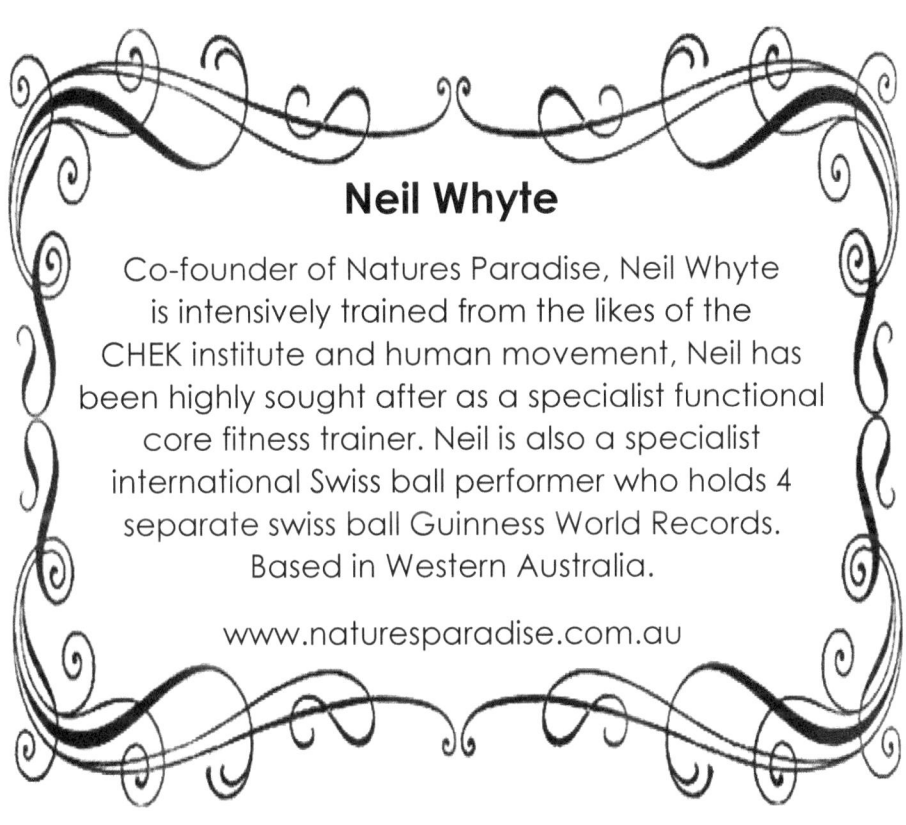

Neil Whyte

Co-founder of Natures Paradise, Neil Whyte
is intensively trained from the likes of the
CHEK institute and human movement, Neil has
been highly sought after as a specialist functional
core fitness trainer. Neil is also a specialist
international Swiss ball performer who holds 4
separate swiss ball Guinness World Records.
Based in Western Australia.

www.naturesparadise.com.au

Reconciliation after abuse: 'How I became friends with my abuser'

~Neil Whyte

1.   What was life like before this happened?

I was just a kid, a talented sportsman and enjoyed many friendships including girlfriends in primary school. I found school work to be rather challenging, my concentration levels at times were poor, and didn't enjoy being in the classroom at times. Instead, I was anxious and keen to get out and play sport as this was my passion and gift.

Today, they diagnose kids like me with ADD, which thankfully I didn't experience and don't necessarily agree with anyhow. Some people develop conscientiousness during childhood/ adolescent years whilst others as adults, and some never. In recent years I have learnt that I developed my high levels of conscientiousness as an adult, as I needed time to mature. Child 'hyperactivity' is far more normal and natural to me than being 'hypoactive'.

2.   Who were you before the attack?

An innocent young boy.

3.   How did it happen, was it someone you knew and trusted or a stranger?

My parents are close friends with Gary's parents for years. He used to babysit me. When I look back I could see how he was 'grooming me' for the moments to arise. We used to have fun for a while and then he would set up these interesting cubby house configurations with blankets etc. Then it somehow seemed to happen. I also remember seeing his father's playboy magazines under his bed, and he used to show them to me.

4.   Did you talk/ appeal to your attacker at the time?

I knew it was wrong, I could feel it, even though I was so young and had no idea about sex of course. Eventually, I had had enough of the abuse, and told him (whilst I was crying) that I was going to tell our parents.

5.   What was their response and attitude?

Once I said I was going to tell my parents, Gary freaked out and begged and cried for me not to tell whilst on his knees. This continued for some time, until I said "Okay, I won't tell."

Gary didn't do anything else after that day.

6.   What's going through your head during the attack?

I pretended that it wasn't happening, but other times he made me do things like masturbate and oral, so it was difficult to ignore.

7.   It finally ends, what are you thinking at that point and what do you do next?

When it finally ended, I just tried to put it out of my mind and get on with my life. I had no idea how many other people this happened to. This was before the social media era, internet and mobile phones.

So, I continued my life, and it was never possible to erase it out of my head because my parents were always frequent friends with Gary's parents.

I always had girlfriends since early primary school, and never once imagined discussing with any of them what happened. I had plenty of good male friends through school and sports, and again, never thought about telling any of them.

This is most likely due to the fact that my life and upbringing never presented itself with any deep and meaningful conversations with anyone, including my parents.

I never felt comfortable telling my parents and it could absolutely tear the friendship apart with Gary's parents. At times over the years I did feel a bit like I was a sacrificial lamb.

When I was a young man playing football to pursue a possible prosperous career, I did have the thoughts come back to me occasionally when we were all naked in the club rooms and in the showers.

I sometimes wondered which of these guys have either 'abused' or 'been abused' themselves. But the reality is, one does not know. It can be a very secretive and private dark space.

I have come to realise though, since the power of the internet and social media, that child abuse and child porn is a bigger problem than I ever imagined. It is obvious that sex, physical and verbal abuse is a major problem. I am not here to speak about women, but the overwhelming majority of the problem, being with men. I think traditionally all too often men are not brought up or trained to share their emotions, but to suppress them.

8. Did you tell anyone: If Yes, who and why and how did they react?

After many years the person I told was my wife. Naturally, she was shocked initially. It took me many years until I told someone, my wife. She is incredibly supportive and can discuss anything, and we often have in depth spiritual conversations.

If No, why? How long before you did tell someone and why?

see next.

9. How did you initially deal with what happened to you?

I simply did my best to ignore it and erase it. Even when it ended, it was so difficult because my parents continued to go out with the same group over the years, so I could never erase it as their names kept popping up all the time. I simply tried to erase it the best I could because I didn't feel like a man at times; it's not the way a tough sportsman should feel. I also had no idea how many other people this happens to.

This all happened pre-social media, mobiles and the internet era, so I had nowhere (to my knowledge) of any support or knowledge on the topic. I wondered if I was one of the 'unlucky ones.

However, in recent years, I have come to terms with the realization that sexual abuse is more widespread than I ever imagined. This has helped to feel like I 'am not alone'.

Just prior to writing this, I celebrated a special birthday with special people who I believe respect me and whom I feel comfortable around. As a part of my speech I told them the whole story. This was another process of 'cleansing' for me and a weight off my shoulders.

Most of all, the aftermath of that, was their overwhelmingly positive response as to how I approached the matter and even more so, how I have ended up friends with him.

10.   Did you blame yourself and if yes why and how did you realise it wasn't your fault?

No. It was absolutely 100% his failed responsibility and duty of care from Gary. He acknowledges that and has taken 100% responsibility for his actions.

11.   What was the defining moment where you decided you would fight for and regain your life?

I had already been warming up to taking action for quite some time, but the clincher was at my mother's funeral where Gary's mother came up to me and spoke for a while. She said, "Remember when Gary used to babysit you?"

I can't begin to tell you how difficult that conversation was for me, and I was so saddened by it.

Anyway, it was this day that prompted me to finally act after nearly 40 years.

12. How do you look at the attack now? Have you forgiven-Why or why not?

The attack now is in the distant past because I took the initiative to present an opportunity for myself and Gary to move forwards. The result out of it all was a result of absolute forgiveness.

13. What was your position on sex after the act and what is it today, did you lose your liking etc for sex or did it come back etc?

I don't believe it influenced my sex life, but I can't be 100% sure.

14. Are there any positives from your situation?

After nearly 40 years ago, the defining moment where I decided to take action to address this matter was when I was at a gathering of friends and family directly after my mother's funeral. I had not seen Gary's mother for years. She came up to me and we had a chat, and she said, "Remember when Gary used to babysit you?"

I can't begin to tell you how difficult this was for me to answer let alone to have a friendly conversation. Soon after, I started to plan my course of action.

First, I had to think seriously about the whole situation. My intuition was telling me that their family is a great one and I wanted no harm. And even though I hadn't seen Gary in nearly 40 years I felt he probably wasn't a bad guy with his upbringing, although that may sound a little presumptuous.

I wanted a positive outcome for both parties. I know this

may sound a little strange to some people, but this is what I wanted.

So, I wrote a letter with an outline of conditions and responsibilities that needed to be met by Gary. As a part of the 'cleansing' and forgiveness aspect, my desire was for him to agree to take full responsibility with a positive outcome by seeing first a psychologist together followed by having lunch together.

Then in the afternoon, my thought was to call upon a wonderful servant of the lord, a chaplain, and good friend of mine. The idea of this second part of the day was for Gary to look into the eyes of god and seek forgiveness, including myself offering that same forgiveness. This was all going to be a part of an opportunity that presented itself to take responsibility and to seek forgiveness, for both of us.

So, my first step was to contact a friend of mine in confidence, and her special partner, for a meeting. First, I had to tell them about the abuse, followed by my plan. I showed her my letter that I was going to send to Gary and they both ultimately supported me 100%. I was to provide Gary the opportunity to take full responsibility first without the need to address any initial formal legal matters. We had no idea what was going to happen, but we looked at possible scenarios 1. He might not reply at all. 2. He replies but is in denial. 3. He could have his lawyer contact me. 4. He contacts me to apologise but doesn't want to go through with the series of requirements. 5. He takes full responsibility and is happy to proceed with the series of conditions.

So, I sent off the letter registered mail to Gary. I still remember the day dropping it in the box, it was a rather telling and nervous moment. I know approximately when he received it via registered mail, and a few hours after receiving it, Gary rang me.

He immediately took responsibility and apologised for everything he may have caused during my life. He even mentioned how he experienced rape at a party a few years after my abuse ended with him. My first reaction here may have been 'karma'. However, I felt that with this happening to him, it could possibly help him understand more emotionally of his own abusive behaviour towards me back then.

We spent 30 minutes on the phone which also included a conversation about his own kids. I then proceeded to ask him how he would feel if this would have happened to his own children. He answered like any normal functioning father should with replies of ''devastation' etc. I could certainly sense his legitimate remorse and regret.

As a part of the series of conditions, Gary was required to book a flight to my state and to then agree with the full day of cleansing and forgiveness.

I must say, considering everything that unfolded, I was remarkably proud of the way Gary went about everything. I couldn't fault him in any way. He even opened up to his wife about it.

Plenty of emotions spilled out from both sides during the first part of the day –the psychologist session. Then in the afternoon I organised a unique session with a very special friend as mentioned, who has been a Minister/ Priest/Chaplain/ Counsellor for 40 years. He organised a private session in his chapel with the most amazing thoughtful organisation and presentation, and I can't thank him enough.

He set up a table that had dead matter of leaves at one end and greenery at the other with candles to be lit to signify new beginnings. Again, emotions spilled out from both sides. I must say, this felt an amazing moment of gratitude and relief through the power of the lord; and that's saying something because I am not a particularly religious person, but rather very spiritual. Interestingly, Gary also said he was very spiritual as well.

So, the last thing to do in the private chapel was to keep a rock each, a symbolic piece of Earth to remind us of the moment forever.

I know how this turned out may appear to be highly unique, but my reason for contributing to this book is to show people that if I can do this, then it is possible for anyone else who has experienced abuse in the past to achieve a similar positive outcome, with the right approach and attitude.

15. How is life now compared to before the attack?

Life was great then and even greater now.

16. Who are you today? I am a constantly developing and learning compassionate human being. My work is to

serve humans to predominantly improve health through a series of wellness coaching and training strategies. It is also important to me to care for the planet, the natural environment and all living species as much as possible.

In closing......

I wish to thank Gary for also writing his part of the story.

I know this outcome between Gary and I may seem highly obscure or strange to a certain percentage of people. I disclosed this story to a client (who had also experienced abuse) when we went for a forest walk, and she couldn't believe (over and over) how Gary and I have ended up friends.

The message I would like to send abroad is the 'potential opportunity' for many others with their own abuse. For me to achieve the outcome that resulted was important for me, because I didn't want to necessarily see the person (Gary) as evil, but a human being that may have experienced trauma in their own life or something else. If one only sees evil, it makes it very difficult to find contentment and resolve.

If Gary denied or failed to take responsibility, then that would have been his choice, and it is his right to do so. Then I may have taken a different course of action, but I didn't have to.

It is important to not let it change the way you are as a person or allowing demons into your behaviour. Abuse in my view still needs to be handled in a responsible sensible manner, as hard as it may seem, and as angry as one may be. Yes, I have had those feelings, but not enough to send me into despair throughout my life, and still managed to remain extremely functional without people even hinting of any abuse.

I do find it rather ironic that there now seems to be in recent months some exposing of alleged sexual abuse of iconic individuals. Is this now the time where men need to express themselves out of the closet?

Why does orange juice come out of an orange when squeezed? Because that is what's inside. You are the orange. When life squeezes you, and in this case, someone abuses you, immediately you want to feel anger, hatred and depression. Then we blame 'that person' for feeling this way, but those feelings were already inside that orange.

So, if you don't want to feel the anger, the hatred or the depression; then we must look inside the orange, so that when life does squeeze you, the only thing that comes out is understanding and love, (Inspired by Wayne Dyer).

If people who are abused can't find mutual understanding and contentment with their perpetrator, then perhaps;

"Always forgive your enemies, nothing annoys them so much."

- Oscar Wilde.

Helena Nista

Helena is a sex & intimacy coach, published author, therapist and speaker. She's a certified sexologist and Tantra practitioner. Helena works with men and women all over the world who want to improve their sex lives. She helps her clients overcome sexual difficulties, become amazing lovers and create mind-blowing experiences in the bedroom.
Based in Sydney, Australia.

www.helenanista.com

1.   What was life like before this happened?

Life was good. But when it comes to my sexuality, I was always very suppressed. I was brought up in a Catholic household. We were very religious, and we didn't talk about sex. Sex was a dirty thing, nudity was inappropriate, and the genitals were a total no-go zone.

The messages I grew up with were "don't go there", "don't touch yourself", "cover up your body, your body is inappropriate, and sex is this horrible thing that nobody even talks about". All that was very harmful but at that stage I didn't have any sex life yet. I was a virgin, I wasn't dating or masturbating.

So, life felt pretty normal. I was going through school and then high school - a Catholic high school.

2.   Who were you before the attack?

I was a very shy and introverted girl. Very ambitious, loving and caring, making big plans for my life, thinking about having a beautiful relationship one day, and a family, and a home, and a career. I really loved French at that stage and wanted to study it. So, I was making plans to be an interpreter or a French teacher.

I was still very religious back then, I was still going to church every Sunday.

3.   How did it happen, was it someone you knew and trusted or a stranger?

I went to France during summer holidays. I was hired as an au pair to take care of two little boys, a one-year-old and a two-year-old. I was staying with the family who took me on holidays with them. They wanted to have some freedom while I was taking care of the kids.

They didn't have a spare room for me in the house, so they put me in a room that was adjacent to the garage. It was on the same property but separate from the main house.

One night, I woke up in complete darkness and I realised that somebody was with me in the room. At first, I thought that I must have slept in for my morning duties with the boys. So, I reached out to look at my clock. I had a big chunky alarm clock sitting next to my bed. But the attacker quickly took it out of my hand, probably worried that I would use it as a weapon.

I was half awake and very confused. I had no idea what was happening. I reached out to put the light on, but the lamp didn't work. I later learned that he unplugged it.

In complete darkness, this man started pulling my covers off and touching my skin. I kept pushing him away and struggling to get him off me. I tried pleading with him by telling him that I had my period and that I was in pain.

It was so surreal! There was a man, a stranger in my room. He just walked into my room and started removing my covers and then my clothes. As I was fighting him off, I kept pleading with him to leave me alone. And he wouldn't, he kept going. The struggle continued, and he must have grown irritated with me because he suddenly pushed something into my arm, it felt like a cold, metallic object. I was told to calm down, or else.

To this day I'm not sure what he was threatening me with, I think it was probably a knife. But back then all I could think of was defending myself. It didn't even occur to me that he could have seriously hurt me. I only knew one thing: I needed to get him out of my room. I needed to get him away from me.

I was so scared... So, I kept fighting. And when he managed to reach between my legs, his fingers encountered the sanitary towel in my underwear. At that point, he must have realized that I really was bleeding. I suppose that my period together with my stubborn resistance, finally made him give up on me. The whole thing lasted about 15 minutes, and then he finally left.

4.   Did you talk/ appeal to your attacker at the time?

I did. I tried to plead with him by telling him that I had my period and that I was in pain. I figured that maybe he would leave me alone if he knew that I was bleeding. And it did seem to help. I can't be really sure what made him walk away in the end. But maybe it was the sanitary towel in my underwear that he encountered while touching my genital area.

5.   What was their response and attitude?

I'm not sure. The only time he spoke was when he pushed that cold object into my arm. Other than that, he was just quiet, he just kept trying to get me to surrender to him. He seemed emotionless to me.

It was completely dark in the room and I couldn't see him. He also pulled his T-shirt up above his nose to hide his face from me. To me, he was just a faceless man.

But obviously, he was scared to be recognised later which is why he was covering his face.

6.   What's going through your head during the attack?

During the attack, all I could think was: "I need to get him out of here", "I need to get him away from me", "I need to keep fighting". That was the only thing going through my mind.

Only once he left, thoughts started flooding my head. I also realized that my body was physically shaking, and the shaking continued for what seemed like a very long time. I was in shock and I was having a traumatic response. While sitting there finally alone, I was starting to realise that this stranger was ready to hurt me in order to get sex.

I kept being bombarded by questions: Are all men like that? What is that about? How can you hurt someone to satisfy your sexual desire? Why is sex such a big thing in the world of men? It was a big thing for me to realise that sexual desire could drive somebody to attack me and to hurt me.

"This was not the last time something like this happened to you. Can you share with the reader?" -Petros

It happened quite a number of times. When I turned twenty, I met my first boyfriend. We were both twenty, we were both studying and living in student houses on the same street. When we started going out together, it was all great and fantastic until we started to have sex.

About three months into the relationship, we became

intimate and from the very beginning, sex was very painful for me. It felt very unpleasant and uncomfortable and I was agreeing to sex more for my partner, than for myself.

I had this idea in my head that sex was for men, for his pleasure, and that, as a girlfriend, I needed to please him, this was my chore, my duty.

It all comes back to the sexual suppression I grew up with and the ideas around sexuality being wrong. Plus, I felt a lot of guilt because I was living in sin - I was having sex with my boyfriend without being married. So, there was all this shame and suppression in my head. And that was really at the core of my physical discomfort during sex. Because I wasn't actually allowing myself to open up sexually, to experience and express my sensuality, my juiciness, my erotic energy.

That part of me was completely shut down, and my partner didn't know how to help me with it either or how to help me become aroused. And he really wanted to have sex! So, he would basically just do it. At times, he would try to give me some oral sex first to warm me up, and only then he would move on to penetration. But, on many occasions, he would basically just lie on top of me and force himself inside of me. My body would often physically shake in pain, while tears were flowing down my face. I kept asking him to stop but he never did until he was finished.

That happened a lot over the course of two years when we were together! Now I know that back then I had a victim mentality, which was due to my wounding and repressive ideas I grew up with. I needed to heal it within myself eventually but at that point I didn't know how to do it, so I just kept attracting men who were abusive.

I didn't even realize that he was raping me... I kept saying "no" and "please stop" but he wouldn't acknowledge it, he wouldn't say anything. He just kept going until he ejaculated, until he was finished.

"And this happened across a number of relationships, is that right?" -Petros

Yes, that's right. With this particular guy, this happened a lot during our two-year relationship. After that, I promised myself that I would never allow it to happen again, but I did. On different occasions, a lover or ex-lover would come to me for sex. I would say "no" and despite that, they would still force themselves upon me, and penetrate me. Back then, it didn't even cross my mind to call it 'rape'. I would think that this partner or ex-partner was desiring me and that somehow, they had a right to use my body for their own pleasure, regardless of how I felt about it.

"You couldn't differentiate between the 'yes' good sex and the 'no' I don't want the sex". -Petros

That's right! Besides, I didn't actually know what good sex was, I never had good sex back then. For me, sex was a painful obligation.

Sadly, I was never raised to be an empowered woman or to claim my pleasure and my body as something beautiful and something that was mine. I always saw sex as a duty and my body as something that I needed to provide to the man in my life.

"Finally, hopefully they end, I imagine at some point it hasn't happened again". -Petros

Yes, there was a point in my life, about five years ago, when I finally drew the line. I was in a 3.5-year relationship with a man that I was deeply in love with. I wanted him to marry me, I wanted to have his child. And again, sex was horrible, but at that point I thought: "that's what sex is." I gave up on trying to make sex anything else than painful or uncomfortable.

"Why was sex terrible cause it seems like even when you were loving and consenting, there was still a sense of sex felt horrible, or is horrible? Apart from the religious upbringing, was there something else that?" Petros

That's a good question, thank you so much for asking it. Now I know how bodies work and

I know a lot about human sexuality. This is why I was able to heal myself sexually and overcome my trauma and wounding. But back then, I had no idea that every time I was saying 'yes' to sex, my body was simultaneously saying 'no, I don't want it'. And every time I forced my body to have sex, I was desensitising my system. And my genital area was sort of armoring itself and energetically withdrawing from sensation to protect me from pain. But at the same time, this armouring was protecting me from pleasure as well.

Every time I was pushing or forcing my body to be open to sex, every time I was opening my legs and opening my vagina to penetration, I was on some level withdrawing from sensation. And I was basically creating numbness and discomfort in my body.

I kept overriding my body's wants and needs and I kept using my head to say "Yes, I am going to have sex right now because he wants to have sex, and it is my role, my duty to have sex right now". And in reality, every single time this happened, I was wounding and re-traumatising my body. So back then, it was almost impossible for me to feel pleasure because my body was so traumatised and numb, and desensitised. So, it really didn't matter if my partner was loving, amazing and caring. He still couldn't give me good sex because my body...

"Because you were blocking it off. Is that what I'm understanding?" - Petros

Absolutely, yeah.

"And it still doesn't give them the right though - if you say no or stop - then that's it. So, it doesn't give them the right. Just to be clear, I don't support what they've done to you." -Petros

That's right, thank you.

So, I was in a loving relationship with this partner but again, he didn't know how to open my body sexually and I didn't know what to do about all this numbness and discomfort I was feeling.

Fortunately, sex with him was very quick. He would finish very quickly, so I was able to just put up with it. Our intercourse lasted between 1 and 5 minutes.

But because of all the pain and discomfort I had endured up to that point during sex, sexual touch was always causing my body to tense up. My system was literally blocking itself and withdrawing from sensation while waiting for the experience to be over. So, there was really no way that I could access my juice and my arousal.

7. It finally ends, what are you thinking at that point and what do you do next?

It all ended with a bit of a bang for me because I found myself in a hospital. My then-partner made love to me in the morning. It was very quick but when he left the bedroom, I suddenly started experiencing a lot of pain in my pelvis.

The pain kept growing stronger and stronger. It would grip me intensely for about 5 seconds, and then it would ease off a little for another 5 seconds. And then it would intensify again for about 5 seconds, etc. I was still in bed, getting more and more scared and confused. I figured that the pain was related to sex because my whole pelvis seemed to be on fire. I was waiting for it to go away but it didn't, so I eventually had to call my partner. It was the worst pain that I had ever felt in my life. I thought that I was either going to die, or that I would never be able to have sex again.

I couldn't get up, I couldn't walk, I couldn't move. I was in so much pain! I asked him to call an ambulance, but he told me that an ambulance could take an hour to arrive while there was an emergency room nearby.

He left the room and I thought: "I can't get up, how am I even going to get dressed?"

I eventually managed to crawl out of bed while the pain kept wreaking havoc in my pelvis. I crawled to my wardrobe and slowly put some clothes on while lying on the floor. I then dragged my sore body out to the front door where my partner saw my convulsed face and finally realized the full extent of my pain and misery. He helped me to the car and we left.

We got to the emergency room at about 6am. It was very early, but there were a few people there already and we had to wait. When the nurse finally saw me, I was told to lie down on a hospital bed. She examined my pelvis, asked a few questions and determined that the source of my pain was a muscle spasm. It turned out that my partner's penis hit a muscle in my bladder, which then started spasming very painfully.

I was given strong muscle relaxants and within 20 minutes the pain disappeared. After that, I was sent home. Fortunately, the whole thing ended well but it was extremely scary for me to realise that sex could put me in a hospital.

And that was my turning point. That's when I realised that I could never have sex the same way again because I could end up in a hospital. That's when I knew that I had to change things, I really had to change the way I had sex. At that point, I had no more choice about that.

"So, before we go down that path, because that going to lead somewhere differently. I want to explore a little bit more - let's say the first incident, second incident when they finished. Immediately after they finish, what are you thinking in all the attacks?" -Petros

"Thank god it's over; thank god I can just go and do my own thing now." Even during consensual sex, I would often think: "oh my god, as soon as he's finished, I can go and read my book, I can go and do something else". Yeah, I pretty much always felt a huge relief: "It's over!"

"And did you think about it anymore after that or did you try and push it away?" -Petros

I always did my best to push it away.

"How quickly did you push it away, after the act?" -Petros

With time, it was getting easier and easier to push it away quickly.

"But afterwards, would you say, you tried to put it away straight away?" -Petros

It depended on the case because I'd had so many different incidents of sexual abuse in my life.

With my first partner, it was an ongoing thing, so I never thought that it was rape, I just thought of it as 'sex'. That's what sex was: horrible, painful, me crying and asking him to stop. That's what sex was.

"What about the first time? The first incident, when it was with a stranger?" -Petros

It took me a long time to get over that. Even that very night, I was sitting there shaking in my bed for at least an hour. Physically shaking and thinking: "What has just happened? How can this have happened? Oh my god, are all men bad? How can people hurt others like that?"

"That's a big difference from a stranger to someone you know isn't it? The thoughts...very different. Want to add anymore to that?"-Petros

I'm just thinking back to my first partner, being raped by him for two years that we were together...

"That one affected you the most, didn't it?" -Petros

Oh absolutely! That really put me on a downhill trajectory with my sex life, which then eventually led to hitting that turning point, the hospital. And then to turning my life around.

But when all that painful sex was happening, there was a sense of hurt, a sense of injustice. I was wondering why I had to put up with it. There was a sense of being broken and damaged. I couldn't understand why I was unable to enjoy sex.

I had seen sex on TV and these lovers always seemed to have a great time. It looked amazing and their bodies seemed to be highly aroused and turned on. Why couldn't I feel arousal, why couldn't I feel the pleasure? What was wrong with me? I always kept bringing it back to this question: 'what's wrong with me?' I was certain that it was all my fault and I just felt inadequate, broken. I felt extremely lonely. I couldn't bring myself to talk to anybody about this because nobody would understand, because people would judge me. And because I wanted everybody to think that I had beautiful, amazing, perfect relationships.

8. Did you tell anyone: If Yes, who and why and how did they react?

I did but it didn't seem to help much.

In case of the original attack, I told my sisters. I spoke to them on the phone because I was still in France, I was still babysitting. My sisters obviously felt bad for me, but they didn't know what to do either. They were very young themselves at the time.

I also mentioned the attack to my best friend in high school. And she helped me to understand what I went through. But I never sought professional help. I didn't really know who to turn to. I was living in Poland and therapy was an unknown concept. You just had to deal with your shit.

In many other cases, I just kept my mouth shut and told no one about what was happening. I felt intense shame that I had allowed something like this to happen to me. And I felt shame that I couldn't enjoy sex.

I felt flawed, I felt that there was something deeply wrong with me. Because back then, I thought that the entire world loved sex. That everybody in the world enjoyed it and had a great time in the bedroom.

I felt like a weirdo. I felt that I was the only person in the world who was broken to this extent, who couldn't work out sex. And that felt terribly lonely.

9. How did you initially deal with what happened to you?

In case of the original attack, I simply tried to forget all about it. I was left with a lot of questions that night and nobody was rushing in with answers. So, I did my best to not think about it ever again.

And in case of the ongoing abuse in my relationships, I tried to deal with it intellectually, to work it out in my head so that I could make changes. I did some research, but my sources of sexual education were very limited back then. I looked for information online and in books, I really wanted to learn what good sex was and how to have it. I figured that if I was having poor sex with every single one of my lovers, then maybe I could simply learn what I was doing wrong.

10. Did you blame yourself and if yes why and how did you realise it wasn't your fault?

Not in every single case. But when the abuser was my partner, I was always strongly blaming myself.

"So, in your original case where it was a stranger, you didn't blame yourself?" -Petros

No, I didn't.

That's interesting. Why? -Petros

I didn't do anything to cause the attack. It was a stranger who came into my room. I was asleep, I wasn't being provocative.

"Which is fair enough too. Do you think if it happened at say a bar or a nightclub?" -Petros

Possibly... There is a lot of victim-blaming in our culture. We ask: "Why did she dress this was? Why was she behaving that way? She should have acted differently". I don't agree with that. I believe that we should live in a society where it's safe to dress or express ourselves in any way we like, without the risk of being attacked. The way someone dresses and acts should never give anybody a permission to hurt them.

"I agree. I just wanted to create a contrast. It was just interesting to see the difference between when you did blame yourself and when you didn't." -Petros

Maybe my sexual abuse story is an unusual one...

11. What was the defining moment where you decided you would fight for and regain your life?

That was right after finding myself in the hospital. On the way back, in the car, when the emotions finally settled, and I wasn't scared anymore. I was sitting in the car very quiet and I kept thinking: "I can't do it anymore. I need to make a change. I need to really change how I do sex." I felt that I finally needed to take control over that part of my life, I needed to fix it.

"What caused you to start thinking like this finally, to say enough is enough after 3-4 attacks?" -Petros

I feared experiencing that intense pain again, of fearing for my life and for my body again. I guess it was a self-preservation fear. If I kept having sex the same way again, I could potentially cause a huge damage to my body or maybe die. It was a huge fear that sex, abusive sex, could push me beyond my limits.

12. How do you look at the attack now? Have you forgiven-Why or why not? see below.

With time, I learned to forgive. I think that a lot of trauma is caused and kept in the body by hate and resentment. So, it's important to forgive, although it doesn't mean that you'll necessarily forget.

13. What was your position on sex after the act and what is it today, did you lose your liking etc for sex or did it come back etc.

The interesting thing is that I always felt a lot of curiosity about sex. And because of that, I was refusing to call it evil or see it as bad. Even though it repeatedly kept causing me pain and discomfort.

At 18, when the first attack happened, I didn't feel a need to think about sex or to bring sex into my life until I had my first boyfriend at 20. And then I had to start thinking about it because my partner wanted to have sex with me. Two years of painful and abusive sex followed.

After that, I really wanted to understand how to experience sexual pleasure, so I started to explore masturbation. And I was trying to look for ways to give myself pleasure, but I was struggling to reach satisfaction. And that's because I was mainly concentrating on rubbing my clitoris. This was resulting in a very quick climax, of only about two seconds or so, and then it was all over. And that experience never seemed very satisfying to me.

So, I kept looking for some sex tips online but almost 20

years ago there really wasn't much out there that could provide me with value. I was still curious, and I played with myself sometimes or had sex with different guys. But it was never satisfying. All by myself, I could give myself some pleasure by touching my clitoris and my genitals. But even then, I only felt a little bit of pleasure followed by a sense of emptiness and disappointment.

Back then I felt very lost, I remained curious but felt like I had no teachers and no tools to learn anything helpful.

"The other thing is that most people have a very; what's the word I'm looking for. A very inaccurate idea of what real sex is too." -Petros

Yes, and so did I! But after getting to the emergency room, I became absolutely determined to find a different way to have sex. There must have been something different than the rushed experience of physical rubbing of two bodies.

After doing some thinking, I remembered the word 'Tantra'. I wasn't sure what it meant but it seemed to me that it had something to do with amazing ecstatic sexual experiences. So, I decided to start there.

That's how my journey of Tantric education and sexual healing began. I was seeing Tantra practitioners, I was reading a lot of books on the topic. I was going to Tantric events and workshops and I was practicing and using all the techniques I was learning about. And slowly I started the process of letting go of this armouring, this layer of numbness from my body and my genital area.

I was finally re-claiming my sexuality and my pleasure. I

was starting to touch myself in a completely new way. I was meeting tantric men and they were making love to me in ways which felt very different and new. I was learning to touch and to be intimate with someone in a way that felt not only pleasurable but also connected and deeply satisfying. The days of porn-style sex were truly over for me...

"Let's be honest, most porn is there to serve the male ego." -Petros

Absolutely.

"Porn really is not, I mean there's some wonderful sex videos out there, but they make up maybe 2% of what's actually out there. Not saying it's good or bad as I think it's both, but porn is not exactly the best example." -Petros

I agree.

"So, you discovered tantra, which is what many on the spiritual path seem to do. You're now discovering this whole new aspect of sex are your feelings now changing, is your body now starting to let down some of that guard?" -Petros

Yes, and it felt amazing. I still remember two sessions I had with a Tantra practitioner in Melbourne who massaged my vagina in each session.

"UM......How did that feel for the first time?" -Petros

Horrible, I was letting go of a lot of pain. The practitioner guided me to release a lot of the blocked wounding and trauma, together with all the anger, frustration and sadness that I was feeling for so many years. Back then, I was holding a lot of stuck energy and stuck emotions in my genital tissue. It was literally blocking my body and my vagina from opening up sexually and from enjoying sex.

Tantric bodywork is very healing. It's about putting people in touch with their bodies, about reclaiming their bodies as beautiful, sensual and erotic. The genitals are covered by a lot of shame and stigma in our society but they're a very beautiful and natural body part. Sexuality is a very natural and healthy aspect of who we are. So, it's about being touched in a way that allows you to reconnect with your pleasure.

As the practitioner was touching different parts of my genital anatomy, she was stimulating the parts of me that were holding fear, numbness, trauma and all the hurt that I experienced. And while doing that, she was supporting me in letting go of all the armouring that I created, all this energetic armour that I formed around my body to protect myself from abusive touch.

During that session, I was screaming in anger, crying in frustration and shaking in pain. I didn't come out of the session completely healed but I definitely released a lot of unhealthy stuff from my body.

Let me show you how this works. Imagine a situation where you're driving a car and suddenly you hit somebody else's car. Nothing happens, you're fine and the other person is fine. You both get out of the cars to exchange details. And now take a moment to think about what is happening in your body at that point - your body is in a bit of a shock, there's fear, there's anxiety, maybe there's frustration. But instead of allowing yourself to feel all these things, we brace ourselves and behave in a 'responsible way'. We don't cry in fear, we don't scream in frustration, we don't give our emotions a true and healthy expression. Instead, we block the emotions, we bottle them up and we step out of the car. We calmly walk over to the other person, check on them, exchange details and get back in the car. We drive home or drive to work and go on with our day or do whatever else we needed to do.

The problem isn't being responsible and doing the right thing. The problem is that we never get to the point of actually relaxing into our emotions, of experiencing and expressing our emotional states in a healthy way. We continue living our lives braced and tense, holding onto the stuck energy of fear, anxiety or anger. And it doesn't have to be a car accident, it can be little things that frustrate and annoy us. But instead of giving them a free, healthy expression, we bottle them up. It's healthy to cry when you're sad, it's healthy to kick a cushion when you're angry. It's healthy to run through the woods if you're feeling frustrated or scream with joy if you're feeling excitement, etc.

Emotions simply need to be felt and released. Emotions are energy in motion that needs to move through us. But we put on a stoic mask and we claim that "everything's fine, I'm fine". "I don't need to cry, I'm ok, I am too busy, I have other things to do right now", etc.

So, over the years, we are storing a lot of trauma, pain

and discomfort, a lot of frustration, sadness, grief, anger etc. because in our society it's not appropriate to give these emotions a healthy release.

"Oh, this just came to mind, not excusing what happened to you, do you think what you experienced was a reflection of what you were feeling about your body and your sexuality, that on an energy level you attracted this? Because It looks like, as bad as what happened to you was, it's developed you into someone wonderful that's ended up somewhere amazing?" -Petros

Oh yes, absolutely. We attract into our lives what we send out energetically. I was raised as a people-pleaser and a victim. I was raised with no self-confidence and with no sense of respect for myself.

There were two levels to my experience. On one hand, I was absolutely attracting these men because a victim will attract an abuser, it's just what they do. If you're a victim, if you emit the energy of a victim into the world, you will attract an abuser to keep you in a state of being a victim.

But on the other hand, relationships with these men were an opportunity for me to heal because they kept showing me where I was suffering. They were pushing me against my suffering and showing me that I was being a victim.

If I didn't encounter all these 'abusers', I would never really have seen my victimhood as well as I did. And I wouldn't have been forced to deal with it, to heal it. So, these relationships were very valuable lessons for me.

14. Are there any positives from your situation?

Yes – deep compassion for other people who go through similar experiences. And a lot of people do! Sexual abuse or discomfort and pain during sex are very common and I have a lot of compassion and understanding for people experiencing it. And I can bring that into my practice as a sex coach but also into my relations with other people.

15. How is life now compared to before the attack?

Amazing! It's been amazing to go through all the sexual education, transformation and healing, to turn around the abuse and to recover from my sexual wounding. I finally learned how to be an embodied person, how to really feel my body and live in my body; how to re-sensitise my entire system so that I can experience blissful pleasure and orgasmic energy just by gently stroking or holding a point on my body. I can now actually experience these states even without being touched, simply by using my breath and awareness...

That was an amazing gift, to be prompted onto a journey of healing, transformation and education about sex. I now have experienced a true sexual low and I know all about the toxic ideas we hold about sex as a society. I witnessed how each generation is hurting the next one when parents install shame and guilt in their children. But I also discovered the other side of the experience, I learned how to be really embodied, connected, sensual and juicy.

Our pleasure potential is absolutely immense and the orgasmic states our bodies are capable of are way beyond anything the society tells you about good sex. And I was able to discover all that because I was so desperate to learn about great sex.

"And I guess it also means that sex is something that is so wonderful and powerful and greater than we understand that, it's not something you need to lose the power of or the love for because of the acts that unfortunately some people do on others. It's more sacred and divine than that." Petros

Yes, but unfortunately our society doesn't really know how to deal with the wonderful power of sex. We have no proper sexual education available. Young people learn from porn, from movies, from the internet.

"Petros: And what's available at school is just not enough either." -Petros

Not at all! We need a much better system of sexual education in our society.

16. Who are you today?

That's a very good question. A lot of different things, but sexually, I'm still on a journey. I don't think I will ever end exploring and delving deeper into my sexuality…

I am a deeply embodied, delicious, sensual goddess, loving my physical experience, loving my body, my sensuality, both with my partner and all by myself.

Heather Morgan

Is a trainer and master practitioner in NLP, Time Line Therapy and hypnosis. Utilising these 3 techniques Heather looks to grow her speaking and help others who have been and are in a similar situation overcome their past. Based in N.S.W.

www.mindmanagementacademy.com.au

1. What was life like before this happened?

When I was little, I was happy go lucky, I guess I was a bit of a tomboy. I loved to play outside in the sun, I was independent, and I guess I got into everything all the time. I did silly things a lot, I remember one time I was home sick from school and I don't know where Mum was, but I decided, I wanted to go to school. I got a frozen bread roll out of the freezer and tried to cut it to make my lunch, but I cut my finger badly. I don't know where Mum came from, I don't really have a very good memory, but I guess she must have come from somewhere. I remember being at school with my finger wrapped up and the other kids thinking I had cut off my finger.

Roller skating and bike riding, running and jumping, I had so much energy and was so full of life. I remember my best friend, we had so much fun together, her name was Megan and our favourite TV show was Grizzly Adam's and we watched this episode where Grizzly Adam's and his Indian friend became blood brothers... So, we decided that it would be a good idea to become blood sisters. Instead of cutting our hands right open, we thought we'd use our fingers, and we became blood sisters.

2. Who were you before the attack?

The first 10 years of my life, I guess, were fun. I didn't really have a care in the world. I went to school and I came home, and I played, I played with my brother and sister. On Sundays I went to Sunday school and my mum would dress me in dresses. I hated dresses, but I had this pretty dress and I don't know how many times I wore it, but it made me feel pretty and I think that's probably when I started thinking that maybe I was a girl.

I used to like to sing, and I think the old lady next door would get sick of my singing. I was quite funny really. I wish I could remember more about my childhood but it's like just little snippets here and there memories about dogs, memories of living in outback South Australia for a little while and then moving to a big town, just trying to remember sometimes hurts my head. I know it was happy and I know I had fun, there were dark days in those early days as well, and I think it seemed that it was all preparing me for what was to come. I know I was free, I know that I was happy, I know that I had fun and I know that I could do pretty much anything I wanted to do.

3.   How did it happen, was it someone you knew and trusted or a stranger?

When I was 10 and I found out that my dad wasn't my dad, I think I thought it was ok because I didn't really understand what was going on and it sounded like fun, having a dad out in the outback of New South Wales and then just after Christmas 1981 I think, it was like an exciting adventure. We were only supposed to go for a month my older sister and my older brother and myself, a month in the school holidays, a month of fun in the sun, a month of meeting new people, a month with a new family, what an exciting adventure.

I was 10 years old and at first, everything was good and one day when it was time to go home we didn't go we stayed. I missed my mum, and we had a baby sister back home, I missed her too, but we never spoke about it. After a while, I'm not sure how many weeks had passed, the local policeman pulled my father over and told him that he had to ring my mum, I don't know what was going on because we were supposed to be back with her.

We went to a phone booth, back in those days that's what you did, and he rang my mum. He talked to her for a while and got my sister and my brother and me to get on the phone and tell her that we didn't want to go back, that we wanted to stay with him and his family. There were two other boys, two more brothers I guess, and a baby on the way, but I still wanted my mum. That's when things changed. I had to be a lady, and I had no idea how to be a lady, I had always played outside, always been one of the boys, always been grubby, loved getting dirty and suddenly I had to be polite and I had to wear dresses and skirts all the time, I hated dresses even more. I don't remember when it first happened, I don't remember the first time he touched me, he was supposed to be my father, my dad, my hero, the man looked after me, that taught me right from wrong, that protected me and defended me and yet here he was being the one to hurt me.

He would do things like make me sit on his lap and touch my chest and then he would say things like "I can't wait for your breasts to grow" he would rub my thighs and at first it was all innocent and easy, I don't remember how it progressed or when it progressed, I have memories of him, touching me, of him measuring himself and telling me what I need to do to ensure that he fitted properly so that he didn't hurt me, of him making me hold his penis, he would make me give him oral pleasure and he would do the same thing to me. I think the worst thing is I can't remember everything, I say I think it's the worst thing because if I could remember then it would make it easier to let it go and forget.

4. Did you talk/ appeal to your attacker at the time or at any time?

For 15 years I was a slave to him in every way and at first, I thought it was probably normal but as I got older and I realised that it wasn't I would beg him to just be my dad, "why can't you just be my dad. Why can't you look after me and protect me?"

I was never allowed to go anywhere, I was never allowed to have a boyfriend, I was never allowed to do anything, even going to school we weren't allowed to leave before 8:30 in the morning and we had to be home by in reasonable time or have a very good reason to be late.

5. What was their response and attitude?

15 years of being the worst person in the world, I was horrible, ugly, fat, stupid, I would never amount to anything and nobody would ever want me. And he told me that every day, 10 times a day. He would make me do stuff to him and he would do stuff to me and he would make me think it was my fault and he would tell me all this stuff that would happen to me if anyone ever found out. If I ever told anyone. He made all of us believe that he was in the army and he was a ruthless killer, he had friends that would find us if we ever left. He told us

numerous times how to kill people, how he could kill someone and make it look like an accident.

6. What's going through your head during the attack?

Sometimes, I thought about doing it to him, how good would it be if I could kill him? How free would I be and the older I got the more I thought about it and the more I thought about killing myself. But then maybe I deserved it, maybe I really was a naughty horrible person that deserved to be treated like this and you know it's hard going through life thinking those thoughts. waiting watching everyone else lead normal lives or what I perceived to be normal I don't know where or when the Happy go lucky me disappeared, the carefree tomboy was buried deep inside me, and the new me was formed. I knew the real me was gone. Every day and I mean EVERY SINGLE DAY! my father had sex with me, sometimes before school, sometimes after school, sometimes he would make me stay home from school, but he always had sex with me.

When I was 15, he made me leave school, I had many ahh……problems, health issues and I had to stay home, which made it even easier for him. So then, sometimes he would have sex with me twice a day. Afterwards, he would try and make me feel better, but only for a little while. I tried to run away, a few times, and boy was that a bad choice.

When I misbehaved, he always used it as an excuse to take me to my room where he would "tell me off" and nobody would come near the room, because they knew I was in trouble again, I would often think, why me?

Sometimes I would think *"could you just hurry the fuck up"*. His mouth and his hands and everything touching my body and I just wanted it over with. I wanted him to leave me alone and sometimes, I would tell him what he wanted to hear and when he left I would cry, I was dying inside, my soul would cry and not a sound would come out.

I wasn't allowed to stay in my room, so I would go outside and find somewhere to hide, if I'd been meant to be doing a task, I'd make sure that task was done! In my mind, I always wished I was dead. Anything in life was better than that, even being dead. I often thought about it how easy it would be, but I was never strong enough, however, if there was one thing that I'm glad didn't happen, I really am very glad that I didn't kill myself.

For 15 years, 15 long, lonely years, I believed I was the worst person in the world, that I deserved everything that happened, I would lose the plot some days, I felt insane crazy some days, some days, I just cried into my pillow, that deep soul wrenching cry, for the innocent little girl, who lost her life for the desires of a sick man.

7. It finally ends, what are you thinking at that point and what do you do next?

I never felt truly happy again until I left at the age of 25, I made my escape, I like to call it my liberation to Freedom, I still never told anyone. I made my escape and disappeared. And then one day I made the decision to tell someone.

8. Did you tell anyone: If Yes, who and why and how did they react? If No, why? How long before you did tell someone and why?

I walked into a big police station in Queensland to a detective there and I made my report. 15 years, across three states, I don't think that young officer was quite ready for what I said, and the detectives had heard nothing quite like it.

Over the years, there were 3 court cases, the first one, in the Northern Territory, was tried with me as an adult, and as such was called consensual, the preceding years were not considered as he had not been tried or convicted, so the fact that I was only 10 when he started didn't even matter.

Then SA and then NSW had their turn, all up he spent, I think, 11 years in jail, and after everything he put me thru, everything he put my sister thru, sometimes I wish I had killed him instead.

When I tell the few people who know that I was 25 when I escaped they seem to look at me a little differently, because they don't understand that although you're an adult you'd been so held down, you drown in everything that you've been told, you believe everything you've been told about yourself and the most difficult thing is to believe that you could actually walk away. So, I hid my past and I never mentioned it, except to the few people that really needed to know because of the court cases that were happening, even then they weren't told the full truth. Its more recent that I can speak more openly about what happened.

9. How did you initially deal with what happened to you?

The next 15 years, I spent scared, "suffering" post-traumatic stress disorder, depression anxiety, panic attacks, waiting for something to happen, living in fear. The friends who know some of my story, often say how strong I am, because of what I went through and how I dealt with it and how normal I seemed on the outside, but they never see the turmoil in the inside.

I put a block on all my emotions, if it hurt my heart, or my head, I would cause physical pain till it blocked out the emotional. Until I was drunk, and I did like to drink, I used alcohol to numb the brain, to shut it up, to stop the thinking, and when I was drunk, it would all come out. I never really did drugs though, I didn't want to lose any sense of, self-awareness and that's what drugs did to you and I guess in a fashion, alcohol does to, but I felt more in control with alcohol than with drugs.

10. Did you blame yourself and if yes why and how did you realise it wasn't your fault?

I did blame myself for a long while. There had to be a reason why it kept happening to me. Trust, love and belief in self were all extremely difficult to deal with, I believed for a long time, that if my mother didn't love me enough to save me from the man she left, then how could I expect anyone else to love me.

I have very little recollection of my childhood even now I've done a lot of healing and a lot of self-growth, self-awareness, I understand now that it wasn't my fault, I understand I never did anything to ask for it and I understand that I wasn't a naughty child or a bad person or even that I'm fat and ugly and horrible. I eventually realised it was my father that had the problem, I was just the unfortunate focus of his release.

11. What was the defining moment where you decided you would fight for and regain your life?

I had to get my life back or lose even more, and I no longer was willing to give anymore, but where to start? They say to forgive is divine, when we forgive somebody, we are not doing it for them, we are doing it for us and to forgive doesn't mean that what they did was right or that you accept responsibility for what they did.

To forgive means that they now no longer have control over you, over your feelings, over your emotions, over the way you react to anything. When you truly forgive, their hold over you are gone and sometimes, people think that you must hold onto a grudge in order to never make the same mistake again however, if you learn from that mistake and accept that everyone makes mistakes, you'll find it so much easier to forgive

12. How do you look at the attack now? Have you forgiven-Why or why not?

The first step in healing your mind and your body, is to accept that what happened, happened, there is nothing you can change. Everything we know about PTSD, depression and anxiety tells us that we must live with it, however we don't. We can just "let it go", we can move forward, we can forgive, and we can, once we know what we need to know, rebuild.

Do I forgive my perpetrator? Do I forgive my father? I have to say yes. He no longer controls me, he no longer controls my feelings, he no longer controls my emotions and I no longer live in fear.

13.   What was your position on sex after the act and what is it today, did you lose your liking etc for sex or did it come back etc.?

I never let anyone get close to me, never let anyone inside my walls, I couldn't trust anyone, not even my husband and it was difficult dealing with my emotions. I blocked everything. Thankfully as I heal I am more able to let in love and the divinity of making love.

I have two children of my own, two boys thankfully. I found it and still find it very difficult to watch my children with men, but I know that I can't draw every male with the same brush as my father. But I was hypervigilant, I was hypervigilant all the time.

14.   Are there any positives from your situation?

To be truly free, to be truly happy, to be the best that you can be, you need to be able to accept what happened, accept that nothing will change it, accept that you had no control over the situation, accept that now however you do have control, you are the one in control, you control your emotions, you control your actions you control your decisions. What happened does not need to rule you and you can grow from it, draining it dry of its strength and not the other way around.

15. How is life now compared to before the attack?

When you decide to be happy, when you decide to move forward, when you decide to be the best that you can be, and you live life, when you smile you show your perpetrator that you are strong, that you are brave and that they have absolutely no control over you anymore. This is my life today, more strength, I have great people in my life, love and I do something I love helping others heal as well. I have my moments, there is work still to be done but compared to how it was once and how it is today......chalk and cheese.

16. Who are you today?

I believe now, that I am a warrior, that I am strong, I fight for me, I fight for mine and I believe that with everything that happened, there is a reason I lived. The strength to fight, to survive and to win, comes from the heart, and the flames may die down, but the fire itself, will never be extinguished. I fight every day, for strength, for sanity sometimes, I fight just to get things done.

As I am healing, more memories return, I am learning how to deal with my emotions, and I try to feel them rather than bury them or hide them with physical pain. My journey started many years ago, and has taken a wide and learning path, I forge ahead, each day, growing and living, knowing that everything that happens, happens for a reason. Everything that I have been thru, everything I have seen, has made me into the person I am today.

"If indeed Goodness is next to Godliness then surely Forgiveness and Love **ARE** Godliness"

-Petros 'The Human GPS' Galanoulis

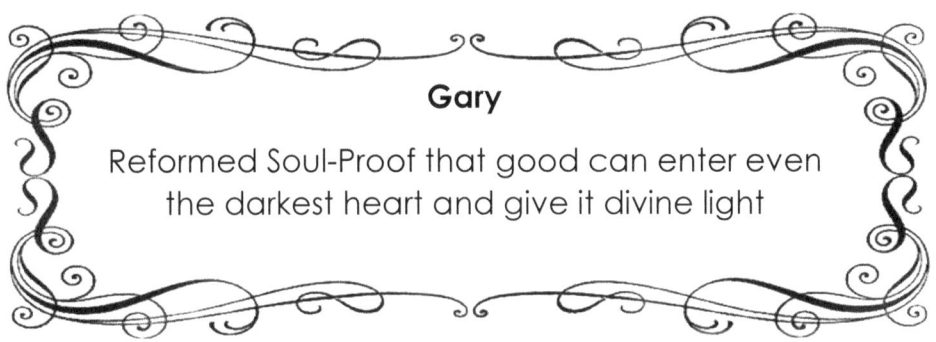

Gary

Reformed Soul-Proof that good can enter even the darkest heart and give it divine light

1. **Were you a onetime offender or multiple time offender?**

One time.

2. **What was life like before you had and eventually caved in to your urges? –**

Normal up bringing from a middle-class family background, but very shy and a somewhat what sheltered / reserved life kept me from making friends both at school and outside.

3. **Where do you believe your urges manifested from and why, what were you looking for?**

On reflection of what I did and the person that I was back then, I believe I was confused at this time with my maturity and truly believe that it was an exploration of nothing more than of my sexuality.

Reflecting now I wonder what would have been the case if I had a larger network of friends of my own age. To clarify this further, prior to me committing this act, my parents could see that I was kind of a closed boy not expressing outwards my feelings much and being somewhat reserved in appearance. So, they had me seen by a few specialist (doctors), who came to the conclusions that while I was a 14-year-old and maturing in my body, I still had the mind of a 10-year-old and acted accordingly.

At the time, this never occurred to me, but in reflecting now and looking back at myself as this 14-year-old boy and what interested me compared to others of the same age, I was totally poles apart in my mind and what absorbed me, and I believe this to be the reason for me not being interested in making friends with others of my age, but towards (Neil, One of the warriors) who was of the age my mind was at.

Additionally, looking back, I did not see this in my mind as an act of homosexuality, and I must say that I have not acted or ever explored this behaviour further after this event. To add further detail, In the following years while I was somewhat rebellious as a teenager to my parents, in my personal life, I was able to hold a steady relationship with my girlfriend at the time and it was not until I was 19 years old did I lose my virginity to same girl (after a 5-year relationship).

Furthermore, throughout this relationship with my girlfriend at the time, there was no feelings of domination or control from my side, and today the way I have lived my life and treated people, loved ones and friends, it has been nothing more than with total compassion, empathy, respect and love. So, as I reflect today on what occurred all those years ago, my mind returns me to the one thought alone and that it was an exploration of my sexuality, it was never to hurt or inflict pain and suffering, but I know my actions to someone Who, was a friend, did just the opposite.

4. Prior to and during, did you have any concept or thought of right and wrong?

At no time was there any thought of right or wrong, it was only during the act when (Neil), told me to stop and threaten to tell my parents, did It hit me (like hitting a wall) that what I was doing was wrong. I remember that I broke down and cried and begged not to involve our parents, so I guess that this was the moment that my brain clicked, and I knew what I did was wrong in so many ways!

5. What was it about your victim(s) that drew you to them?

As indicated in an above statement (question / answer 2), not having a large social network of friends at school, plus where my mind was. It was affection & friendship, that drew me towards (Neil), as I saw him as someone that I could connect with. While we did not see each other regularly, I did look forward to the times when we did get together either at the football or at each other's homes listening to music and playing air guitar to ACDC!

6. Why did you do what you did?

I guess this is the question that is always asked when someone commits an act that I did to someone I consider as a friend.

In reflection, I don't have an answer for it, and it's the main question that I keep on asking myself today when I reflect on my actions and the pain that I caused, but I still come back to the same answer? Is there one straight answer, I don't know?

7. What were your thoughts and feelings after the act(s), did you get what you were after?

As per my comments in question 4, my feelings were of being scared and confused all at the same time. The threat of our parents being involved took over and any feelings or thought I may have had with regards to what I was looking for / after.

8. Did you feel remorse, or did that come later if at all?

Again, like my answer in question 4&7 at the time it was more of being scared and confused, but also of wrong doing. After the event, we never saw each and over time without our parents being involved, I forgot about what occurred and thought it was left at that.

It was not until last year (2016) when I was contacted that remorse hit me like a ton of bricks. I feel remorse, guilt, ashamed and disgust in what I did every day, and while I never shied away from owning up to what I did when I was contacted.

The biggest remorse that I have and will take with me for the rest of my life, is that I did not know how effected (Neil) all this time was. Nothing I can say will ever cover the pain of my actions 38 years ago and if I had known then what I do now, I would have done whatever was needed to be done and would have worked with (Neil) to confess and seek forgiveness for what I did.

9. Many victims blame themselves for being attacked, is that in anyway right, should they blame themselves or is this entirely on you the offender? Why so?

Never! should a victim ever blame themselves for being attacked, you hear this comment all the time and this is something that is not true, the only person ever to blame is the person that commits the act, and for this act, that was me! and I'm the only person who is to blame!

I know this to be true, because I also fell victim to an act of abuse some 6 years later and while I suppressed this and kept it to myself for 25 years before telling anyone, I never once blamed myself for what happen to me, so again to answer your question, no victims should ever blame themselves. Many in society like to forward or place the blame in part to the victim, by the way they acted at the time etc, but this is not true, as for me the blame lays 100% at the feet of the person who committed the act.

10. Do you genuinely now see the wrongness of your way, how-why?

Every single moment of my day and life I reflect on this. As you can see and read from my answer before and after this question, you can view my heart filled sorrow of my actions and also how I live my life and treat others.

11. How do you know you are healed in that you won't commit such an act again?

I believe the way in which I have lived / conducted my life since this act all those years ago, is proof that I'm healed.

I have not ever once since that time, ever had a thought or committed an offense or even dominated anyone in my life. I believe that I have truly lived and continue to live, a healthy, respectful, safe, compassionate, fun filled life with love and cherish for life and all around.

12. What is your view now towards sex and the gender you offended on?

Sex is expression of life that is shared between two

people that love one another and should be cherished by all and not used as a weapon to dominate or hurt another, but a gift between parties who can confide in each other to bring joy and happiness to their lives. To me gender does not play apart, it's love, respect and affection that are the key towards a healthy sexual relationship.

13. If you could say something to your victim and their family, what would it be?

After being approach by (Neil) some 38 years after my inexcusable event, I was blessed to be asked to be part of both counselling and a very special and personal spiritual ceremony, where I could confess and take responsibility for my action and seek forgiveness for what I did so many years before. Since this ceremony some 16 months ago, the ritual still resonates within me like a fire within my soul, and not in a negative way, but one with a power of sincere love and respect for life, but one also of never forgetting what my actions all those years ago caused to someone I consider a friend.

One thing, I will be forever grateful from this confession and cleansing ceremony, is that I have rekindled a friendship with (Neil), which is something that way back when I committed this despicable act, I should have seen the light not to have harmed someone that I saw as a friend, as one thing that friends should never do is harm one another, ever!

While I'm not religious, I do see myself as a spiritual person and every morning that I wake since being part of the ceremony, I take a quiet moment to say a special prayer and thought to (Neil), apologising for both my actions and pain and suffering that I have caused. I have also made a promise to myself that I will for the rest of my life ensure that every morning I will continue to make this prayer as a further sign of my remorse and seeking for forgiveness.

In my line of work, I'm fortunate to travel constantly, and I visit places around the world where there is different cultures and religions. In my spear time at these places (and again since having this ceremony with (Neil),) I now take the time to stop and soak in a more spiritual atmosphere especially at places like parks, churches, open areas of nature and just looking at people as "one". While as I mentioned in pervious answers I have lived my life in a happy, healthy, loved filled way, I now also see the world in a stronger spiritual way, where compassion & forgiveness is everywhere as long as people are truly remorseful for their actions today and in the past.

14.   Should they ever forgive you?

From compassion comes forgiveness, and during our ceremony I asked and sought forgiveness for my actions, to which I did receive. I know that gaining forgiveness for what I did is not easy nor is it something that will occur overnight nor should it. But it's a journey forward towards understanding and trust with one's actions that ultimately deliver forgiveness.

15. Have you or will you forgive yourself?

Since taking part with (Neil) in a very moving ceremony, I have come to forgive myself for the inexcusable act that I committed on someone that I was taking care of and viewed as a friend, however I will never forget or ever make excuses for what I did *(Ever).*

PART 2

Rising from the darkness and reaching for the light.

13 Steps to Healing, Forgiveness, Self-Reclaim and Empowerment.

FREE VIDEO: A WARRIOR's ROUND TABLE.

What does forgiveness mean today? Is the saying 'forgive and forget' an absolute lie because after all do you ever truly forget? Can you? SHOULD YOU?

Why and how did the warrior's do it, how did they forgive their perpetrators for their most heinous act?

Watch this bonus video of a 'virtual round table' discussion that I have with the warriors as we explore what is forgiveness and its modern-day implications, what does it mean to forgive and what it means for you and me to have forgiveness despite all that is going on around us in the world.

http://www.yougotthismentalhealth.com.au/warriors-talk

**Join Us For Exclusives In
The Reaching For The Light Facebook Group**

Share your favourite parts of the book

Your inspiring story

Support

Great interviews

Insightful and exciting videos,

Events,

Competitions,

Specials plus more.

www.facebook.com/groups/reachingforthelight

"The good news is we choose whether to be eggs or coal when under life's extreme pressures and turbulence. Where one is completely crushed, the other becomes a diamond"

-Petros 'The Human GPS' Galanoulis

Petros' Notes

The steps I am about to share with you are 13 steps that over time I have partly developed and combined with existing work and used on myself and others and that have consistently shown positive effect. Although in the context of this book I focus them on healing from rape and sexual assault, they can be used to heal from any trauma or loss. They are not all there is out there but what I have found to be consistently and highly effective over time.

These steps do not reflect a particular modality of therapy, there are many of those and you can certainly explore them and see what works best for you. What these 13 steps are is a process, they are a powerful series of experience that may lead you to feeling healed, whole and empowered once more or even for the first time. They help you to take the positive and the wisdom from your experience and turn that in to life experiences that you can build a great or greater life on in due course.

Some things I need to let you know that are important

are that time is not a factor, time is irrelevant, the healing and growth will take however long you need and that is up to you.

Secondly it takes effort, persistence and resilience, healing etc is simple but not easy, simple in that you do, for example, these 13 steps and you get better, in practice though it requires something from you and progress happens accordingly. Let me assure you there will be tough times and times where you will go backwards, however in each fall/ failure there is a lesson that when realised helps you move forward so embrace those moments

Finally I can't express enough how magical and effective and therefore important it is that during your powerful journey to not just be a participant in it, a character in the story but to as much as possible be an observer of what is happening within you and around you and be inquisitive, seek answers, this helps massively with the anxiety and depression that comes with loss and trauma etc.

The biggest lie you can believe in these moments is that you can't overcome tragedy and that that's life and how it is, NO, that's one way life could be BUT there are other choices to, it's up to you and I share with you, should you choose to reclaim your life and live it the best you ever have, how you can do it with the following 13 steps *(Please note they can be done in any order)*.

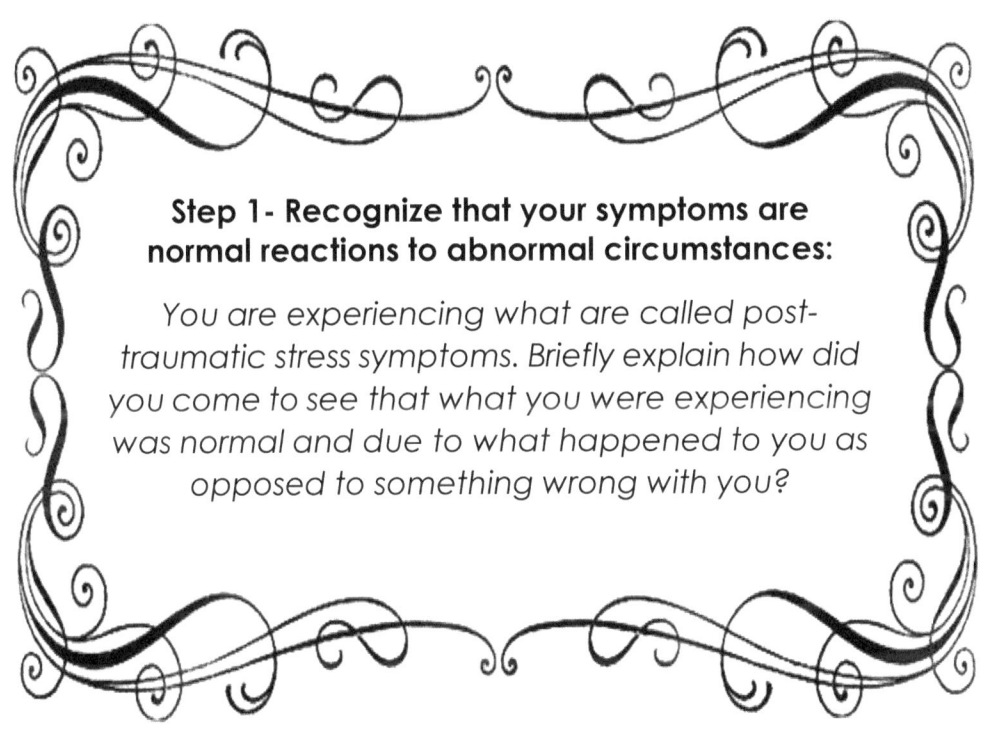

Step 1- Recognize that your symptoms are normal reactions to abnormal circumstances:

You are experiencing what are called post-traumatic stress symptoms. Briefly explain how did you come to see that what you were experiencing was normal and due to what happened to you as opposed to something wrong with you?

Gunther:

When I heard about post-traumatic stress disorder for the first time, I did not relate this mental condition that results in a series of emotional and physical reactions; to my own traumatic events. I have heard the term used in relation to the military and only later in my life understood that it also applies to survivors like myself who have experienced trauma through sexual abuse.

Now, looking back I understand that I suffered under PTSD. Particularly during the long term of my sexual abuse, I suffered immense physical pain. Such as headaches, dizziness, fatigue, chest and heart pain, breathing difficulties in my chest, and stomach and struggling with digestive issues. Even until this day some of those physical pains have not left me completely. Probably hyperarousal, which is having difficulty falling or staying asleep, is still haunting me to this day.

Only in the last decade have I accepted that it is perfectly normal to have experienced uncharacteristic feelings of fear, guilt, stress, anxiety, poor self-esteem, nervousness and depression. Those feelings were sometimes very extreme and caused me difficulties to function appropriately in everyday life. Only after counselling, meditation and self-development courses have I been able to accept, learn, grow and move on from my PTSD. Since I have processed my memories, I have learnt techniques to cope and create a better life each day. I do not live in the past - I live in the present, which gives me the opportunity to be all I want to be.

Helena:

It's when I started studying tantra, and I was going to all these workshops and events and speaking to all the other people that I finally started to learn about the sexual reality of other people in the world. And then I took it even further when I started coaching people and working with people myself as a tantra practitioner. And they were telling me their stories, and I finally realised that 'oh my god, barely anybody has got a good, satisfying sex life.' And a lot of people struggle with either discomfort or frustration or with these subconscious or limiting beliefs that push people to have sex when they don't want to or, suppression that can push people to be aggressive sexually or be abusive sexually. So, this is a reality in our society and a lot of people struggle with that.

"So, what I take from that is, initially getting out there and researching. And you even grew your recent learning through others' experiences". -Petros

Helena: Exactly, yeah. Hearing or being in a circle of people where everybody's wanting to learn about sexuality and sacred sexuality and tantra, and hearing about their own experiences with sex. And realising, 'I'm not the only one, I'm not a weirdo that struggles with sex, and has experienced sexual pain and abuse.' I am just one of the many people who have.

Kylie: This is one of the harder things. I was so jumpy to start with, paranoid and uneasy. I knew it was a normal thing and that only time would help let it settle. Again, I think I was very lucky that I could accept and move on as I did. I talked to myself a lot when I was having an episode, deep breaths and say that I was safe and that it wasn't his car etc. That he couldn't hurt me.

Neil: I was too young to understand at the time, however as an adult yes, I see that what I have experienced is perfectly normal for the circumstance and part of the process.

Heather:

I don't know that's a really hard question to answer. When did I realize? I think I always knew that because of what had happened to me, what I'd been through, I've always been one of those people that kind of thought- *you're not sent a trial that you can't overcome.* So, I always had a sense that everything that I'd been through and everything that I was feeling was part of that learning process for me.

The emotions were probably the hardest thing to deal with because, and even now, I suppress a lot of emotions, so I didn't feel emotionally connected to anything or anyone because I blocked all of those. I would have anger sometimes but then that'll manifest in other ways, in like fear of heights, fear of spiders I guess all those kinds of fears/ phobias and panic attacks which I also knew; I guess, was because of what I'd been through. Like my fear of the dark I knew was because not of anything being wrong with me as such it was because of what I've been through.

John:

It is hard to suggest that I particularly felt that there was anything wrong with me because of the sexual assaults directly. I was convinced there was a whole lot wrong with me because I was deeply unsettled living in an alcoholic home in which there was a substantial amount of tension. Both my parents for each of their reasons had become withdrawn and distant. My father was pre-occupied with his own issues and I suspect dissatisfaction with his own life and my mother had retreated behind a literal wall of romantic novels. There were many occasions where I would attempt to talk to my mother but her irritation at being brought back into the real world and away from the books whose covers always had an excruciatingly handsome man looking deeply and dominantly into the simpering eyes of some damsel that clearly needed rescuing by him from whatever ghastly circumstance had afflicted her.

Reaching my 20's with the cumulative effects of sexual assault, a deep personal dishonesty and a crushing certainty of my isolation in this world led to a deeply held sense of self-pity which was singularly the most destructive component of my psyche.

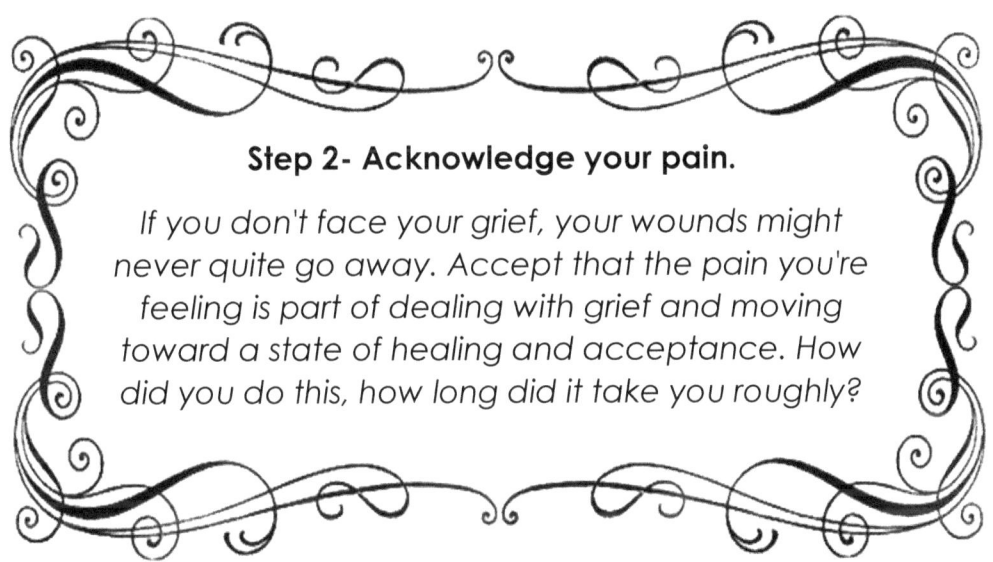

Step 2- Acknowledge your pain.

If you don't face your grief, your wounds might never quite go away. Accept that the pain you're feeling is part of dealing with grief and moving toward a state of healing and acceptance. How did you do this, how long did it take you roughly?

Gunther:

Every wound creates pain and it takes time for it to heal but heal it will if you let it. How long does this process take you may ask? Well, how long is a piece of string? Having spent half of my life in a cult and being sexually abused for over twenty years taught me to face my own Demons. My Demons represented fears, guilt, worthlessness, anxiety, depression, anger, doubts, negative beliefs and limited decisions. These were the source of my sufferings or pain you may call it. Once I understood that everything I desire lies on the other side of facing my Demons/Fears I started to breakdown those negative emotions to experience the greatness I knew I deserved. Think about it, what are those Demons in your life, in my life they were only my own illusions.

Brendon Burchard writes in The Motivation Manifesto: "Our internal demons poison us with worry and fear whenever we might be vulnerable, stunting our growth and vitality. Our destiny is decided by how well we know our demons of Doubt and Delay, how well we defend against them, and how many battles we win against them each day of our lives."

Facing my demons is part of my life. When things are particularly rough, it may seem as if the demons are winning. But as long as I am still living and breathing, I am the victor. In the last few years I have learnt techniques which deal with those inner Demons as soon as they show their ugly head. Therefore, I decide daily not to feed my inner Demons and be the victim of my past story, but focus on my dreams and goals, and the only way to attain them is to never give up, no matter how much we may feel like it.

Helena:

How long did it take me to acknowledge my pain? Or how did I do it?

"How did you get to that point? And say- "you know what? I'm not going to push this away, I'm hurting, and I accept that I'm hurting". -Petros

Helena:

I guess on- going, it was just my reality that I couldn't quite become...keep myself blind from it anymore. So, I was aware of my pain for a very long time before I started to deal with it and heal it, but eventually I realised the power of acknowledging the pain.

Kylie:

I ran from the pain for a little while, the pivotal point for me was when I had a man in my bed for the first time, I simply could not sleep, he ended up leaving rather early in the morning. That was the moment I knew if I ever wanted to be close with someone again I would have to deal with the pain. This would have been about 2-3 months after the attack. Facing the pain was hard, I sought counselling and that worked to a degree. I listened to all the motivational speakers and inspirations, which was something I was used to anyway. By finally acknowledging the pain, I was able to start pulling myself out of the darkness and start breaking slowly the shackles of my situation.

Neil:

It took nearly 40 years before I finally decided to act and confront the reality. I pretended it never happened mostly. The problem over the years was I could never erase it as my parents remained very close friends with his parents, thus I always heard their names.

Every 10 years I got a little angry about it. As time went by, and the digital era came in our world, I realized I was not alone, not by far and it was time to face it, if I was to save myself.

Heather:

It took a long time because everyone's always said to me how strong I am, and it was difficult to acknowledge that I was in pain that it hurt, that you know I shouldn't have been blaming myself and yeah quite simply because I was such a strong person. If I'm that strong why am I not dealing with the pain?

So, to be able to say, "no wait it does hurt", took a long time and that was probably that defining moment when I saw the truck and I went oh my god that's like you can't do that you know. You must accept that you need help, you have to accept that the pain is real, you have to accept that everything that you've been through is what you are now and why you are suffering.

So, I guess from that point of view that defining moment was when I looked at the shiny red truck and thought time to fix all my problems.

Heather:

Absolutely, yeah when I was looking at that truck and I went "oh my god" like you have to be able to accept. It doesn't matter how strong you are, it doesn't matter what you've been through you have to accept that you have been through that trauma and in order to help release it you need to understand that it is pain, that it is real, that it did happened, and you can get past it!

John:

"Resentment" is an interesting word. It is an amalgam of two words, the "re" part suggests the notion of repetition the "sentiment" part refers to the senses. I suppose it has a Latin root because many words in English dealing with feelings use the "sen" prefix, "sentient", "sensible" and "sensory" to name a few. In essence the word "resentment" means to "re-feel" something.

It became a very corrosive force because I wouldn't re-feel something once or twice, I would do it again and again and again and on each occasion as I sipped from that well it would distil into a deeper and deeper feeling purified each time round with the spiritual carcinogen that would be the final product.

Again, and again until the knot churning in the pit of my stomach would tighten with such intensity that the physical act of breathing became a labour. That was the spring of my self-pity. The black morass that I could draw

168

from like some Golem sneering at the world around me both petrified and secured by the isolation of my anger, jealousy and loathing of others. It was as if I lived in a cold emotional dungeon, barren and secluded, with a slit for a window by which I could judge others but an oubliette that gave no comfort in its occupation.

Step 3: Actively grieve and mourn.

Grief is an inner sense of loss, sadness and emptiness. Mourning is how you express those feelings. You might plan a funeral or memorial service, wear black, and carry a somber demeanor. Both grief and mourning are natural and necessary parts of the healing process after a loss or crisis/ trauma. How did you grieve?

Gunther:

How did I grieve the loss of self and all that is associated with not wanting any more pain?

I believe when you are abused as a child, whether you know it or not, your innocence is stolen away from you. A piece of your childhood is gone. The innocence that I felt entitled to have, is no longer mine to have. I guess, it is only natural that one would feel the loss from that.

Being sexually abused as a child is feeling a kind of loss of "what could have been". Many times, in my life I have wondered what kind of person I might have been if I had never been abused! I certainly would not have some of the anxious behaviours that I do now! Does it mean that I wouldn't have "Problems?" Probably not! No one is perfect, we all have our own issues, but I know for one that I would probably feel different about my self-esteem.

Is it easy? Absolutely Not! Grieving Hurts! I guess this is why so many people avoid it and get stuck in denial! So, what I realised is, that if I never deal with it, I might never be able to be fully happy or at peace with myself. It means going through the grieving process no matter what. In my case I started seeing a counsellor, I was also talking with someone I knew and trusted, getting involved with my hobby and joining a swimming club, talking to my partner and sharing my story with strangers.

Basically, I went through different stages which led me to Denial then Anger, Depression then Anxiety, Worthlessness then Self-doubt and finally, Acceptance then Responsibility which enables me to move forward in my life.

The desire that I wanted to heal and grow gave me the necessary strengths of the healing process after a loss. I want to help myself and in turn help others, though at times it feels like one step forward and three steps back. Acknowledging that the past is past, and to live in the present moment is the key. Which in return has empowered me to forgive myself and others.

Helena:

That's a good one because before I entered the tantric part I had no idea how to do that. I was just holding all that pain and grief in my body and I didn't' even know what I'm supposed to do. Like I did mention there was no therapy around and especially back in Poland. I didn't know, I was just holding it all stuck inside, but when I started studying tantra and I learned that there are tantric practitioners that can help you, I started having sessions. And having experiences of grieving and mourning during events when we would perform healing activities on each other in pairs. And that's when I first started to give my pain a voice. And I would scream in frustration and I would cry, and cry and cry and I was just releasing finally and mourning all this time that I was put through pain.

"WOW, I can feel the intensity" -Petros

Helena:

It was intense. I learned that sex itself can be very healing because having sex with a loving, caring, gentle partner was touching on all these energetic moves inside of me and I cried pretty much every single time during sex for about a year and a half. And my partners knew- different partners during that time just knew that it was nothing to do with them. It was just me releasing my trauma and my pain. And every time there was sexual touch involved I would feel a rush of sadness or grief, I would just allow that. Finally, I was allowing myself to express that grief and mourn the pain.

"Do you think it coincidence that healing process, the intensity, is equal to the intensity of an orgasm? Coincidence, or are they related?"   -Petros

Helena:

They are very related, oh my god. I never thought about it this way, they are very related.

"You see things very differently to other people, so that's why I come up with some strange questions". -Petros

Helena:

I love it! Because, yeah, you think about it and orgasm is just a release of that intense sexual energy. It's just a release. You've been building up, building up and then, poof, suddenly this amazing, pleasurable intense release happens. And when it comes to this, all this grief and years of holding onto your pain and frustration and wounding etc. to finally let it out, it's quite orgasmic. Absolutely.

Kylie:

I was somber for a period, indeed, I felt empty most of

the time but pushed on. I cried and cried and felt helpless and frustrated. I let myself feel these as they needed to be felt which I think helped a lot. I was already being brave, bottling anything up wasn't going to help. Let it out, give yourself the gift of grieving and mourning, it's really the first physical step to healing and empowerment.

Neil:

During both sessions with the psychologist and Bruce (Chaplain), I was very emotional, so was my now friend, former perpetrator. It was very heartfelt, satisfying, relief, mutually rewarding. I never felt like this over the years, just a bit angry at times, never emotional with tears. Leading up to our Day of Reconciliation, I was getting quite emotional and this was necessary as it helped with getting to the next step of the journey, the process.

Heather:

I don't think I did.

No? Did you ever? -Petros

Heather:

No.

That's interesting, why do you think that is?   -Petros

Heather:

I don't know, I just don't think I ever have. I....

"Has that affected your ability to put this behind you in any way?" -Petros

Heather:

I don't think so.

That's very interesting, so you have acknowledged the pain, how did you deal with it? -Petros

Heather:

Acceptance. I've been it happened to me and I guess 15 years of having to deal with it and then another 15 years accepting it. So, for me it felt more like acceptance, it happened I can't change it there is nothing in this world that that will ever change it and even if I could I wouldn't and I think that was the thing I know for an actual fact inside heart brain whatever I wouldn't change a single thing simply because of my two children and I know if I changed one thing I wouldn't have my children because I would be a different person.

You know if one thing didn't happen to me then I wouldn't be who I am now, where I am now with my children, I would be a totally different person. So, you know like I may have had other children but I wouldn't have my boys and I would not change that for the world so I think it was more of an acceptance that we'll go through different things in our life to teach us so that we can learn and grow and from that I accept everything that I've been through, everything that happened to me because I am who I am because of that.

"So, we could sort of say practicing acceptance and being able to look at the end result meaning where you're at now perhaps that was your process?" -Petros

Heather:

Yeah, I guess it was.

John:

If there was grief, then it took the form of self-pity. I had convinced myself that I was a misunderstood genius of such deep and profound intelligence that no one could understand me. I was, in my humble opinion, a latter-day Oscar Wilde, witty to the core and splendid in my cleverness. If only other people could see it. I had never produced a single useful work and it wasn't genius that I possessed but rather anger at others' honesty.

Nevertheless, it was the honesty of another that saved my life. Standing near a bar one evening I was regaling a lady with my wit and wisdom on some topic or another and I was feeling particularly superior as I listened to my own cleverness. At one point in the conversation she stopped me and said,

"Goodness me I hear you, and do you know what you are?" she asked with an impressed smile.

"Aha.", I thought to myself, finally a recognition of my brilliance so I prepared myself to be heralded as a truly witty and clever person.

"Go on, what am I?" I replied waiting for the recognition I so long awaited.

"You're a fuckwit." she said with a measured look in my direction.

I was utterly shattered. She had struck me amidships with

a torpedo. At that moment I was expecting high praise I received a galling criticism. Perhaps on another day it may not have concerned me in the least but at that moment it was utterly devastating. What made it so devastating was its honesty. There was no denying the truth of it. It made me crumple and it was the beginning of the end of so much of what I had become.

My use of alcohol had by this time also become a major problem. On the 29th of September 1986 I got really drunk and with one thing leading to another I fell from the air-conditioning system in the Darwin Casino. Don't ask, long story.

As I was an operational police officer at the time (in fact I was relegated to communications where I suspect the police force was trying to keep an eye on me), it was not a good look. It was also the darkest place I ever have been to before or since.

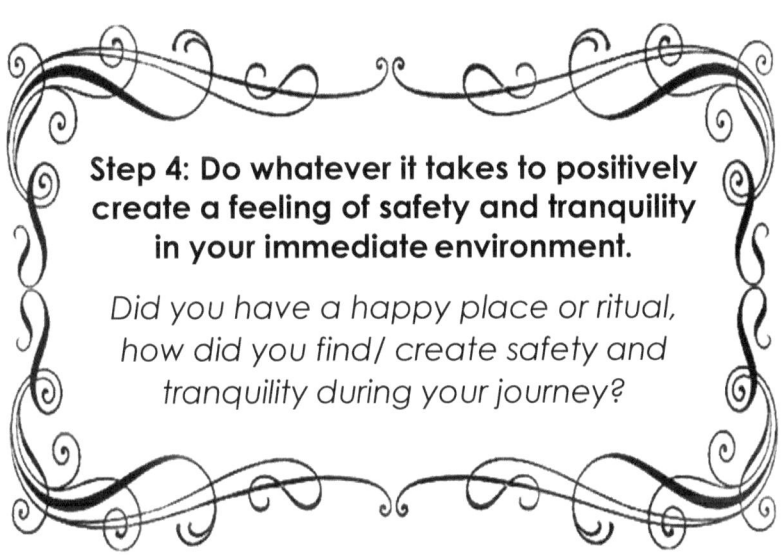

Step 4: Do whatever it takes to positively create a feeling of safety and tranquility in your immediate environment.

Did you have a happy place or ritual, how did you find/ create safety and tranquility during your journey?

Gunther:

All things being equal, I have had, and still have, several things where I find my serenity. Being a passionate swimmer since the age of ten I believe healthy exercise has given me physical strength and worked wonders for stress relief. Despite the chlorine, there's a certain feel-good factor that comes from swimming in a pool. In my opinion swimming has therapeutic qualities which aren't limited just to the physical exercise.

Since I was part of a religious cult, meditation, prayer, and spirituality throughout my years has provided me an unshaken peacefulness. The quietness and silence that one experiences during meditation gets you into a place of disposition free from stress. It is hard to describe but I find my emotional serenity in those moments.

I also love reading books, one could perhaps call me a book-acholic. There is never a time when I do not read a book. One of my favourites authors during my time of abuse was Joyce Meyer (https://en.wiGaryedia.org/wiki/Joyce_Meyer), her story resonated with me and gave me hope in a hopeless situation. Getting in touch with books that are helpful and useful to read when facing certain problems, believe me can be very therapeutic. I read books to live a better life and to approach any situation more wisely then yesterday.

Well, what would life be without coffee? Many times, would you find me alone in a coffee shop or with the coffee in my hand at a remote place pondering about life, while enjoying a taste of 'Heaven'. Since leaving the cult, I have attended a lot of self-development courses. I also enjoy hanging out with my family and friends on a regular basis.

Helena:

Having my own place was big for that because I was finally on my own, and I didn't owe sex to anybody. And I was actively reversing that kind of thinking. So, I was on my own and I had lovers at that stage, beautiful tantric men but I had my own space and it was my sanctuary. And I knew that I was safe in there.

"So, for the people who can't afford to rent or buy a home, the equivalent to what you're saying is 'find a space where you control who comes in and out."-Petros

Helena:

Yeah, exactly. And it might even mean as much as being single for a little bit, so you don't feel like you owe sex to anybody, because women can feel like that. My partner or my husband needs sex, this man needs sex, so I owe him that, I need to give him that. But I'm not saying break up with your partner if you're in a beautiful relationship but, you know, having space or time where you can be fully respectful and honouring of your own body and your own need.

"Which is very important because so many people just don't do that. In fact, I would say maybe 90% or 95% of people these days don't do that". -Petros

Helena:

Well the experience of having my own home back then was extremely healing and I stayed there for two years.

And I had full control over who is there, who is not there. It was my sanctuary, it was my kingdom and I was safe in there. And I was meditating a lot to reclaim that beautiful peace, that inner peace that I know I didn't want to live in frustration or grief anymore.

Kylie:

I spent a lot of time in nature, near waterfalls. I would lie in bed and say thank you for my day and to ask to keep me safe while I slept. I wore angel pendants for Michael and Gabrielle, protectors and angels of strength and peace. Listened to music – Demi Lovato's 'skyscraper' and the song 'fight song' got me through a lot.

Neil:

The place in which it was a fantastic bonding of spirituality and relief, was with my good friend and chaplain (Bruce), when we were all together in church. Both Gary and I kept a rock to symbolise the moment that we both went through.

Heather:

The gym. I found that I started going to the gym probably a couple of years ago and then in the last 12 months mostly it's become my happy place, I go there heaps, even this morning on my day off I still went to the gym because it gives me that sense that I can I can do anything there. So, you know, and I can think my own thoughts and feel my own feelings and I don't have to worry about anyone it's just me, it's my place.

Yeah and if I do go, because like my gym here is small so

generally it's just me, there's no one else there. So yeah, it's really good, so if I am feeling negative it doesn't matter because any negative thoughts that come up even if I do end up having a cry you know there's no one there anyway so I can just push through it.

John:

It was about changing habits and changing mindset for me.

"Deep thought" was a large rock that was on some cliffs in Darwin. As I was taking steps to recover I would jump over the fence around the cliffs and Deep Thought a craggy section of the cliff that had separated itself from the rest of the cliff face. To get to it you had to step over a small fracture in the rock, but it offered an uninterrupted view of the setting sun over Darwin Harbour.

I visited Deep Thought every single day for months. It was a place of quiet solitude and a place I could safely get lost in thoughts and think about the many things in my life that had to change. That rock was a place that enabled me the opportunity to digest my fears and process the absurdity of my resentments. The thunderstorms that roll across Darwin Harbour added drama to the scenery and those tempests often reflected my own mind. Often, late in the year the storms would come and then peter out. As they dissolved, they took my anxieties with them.

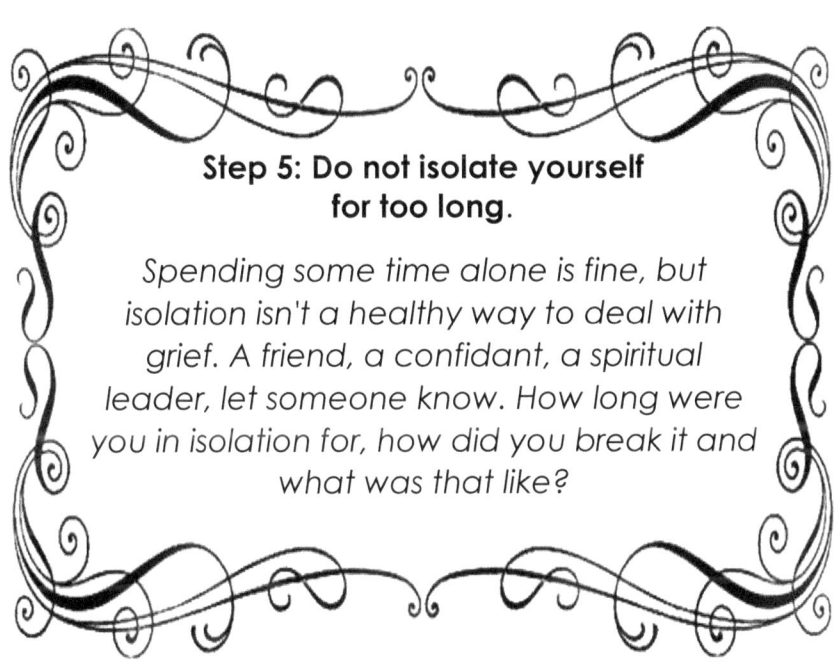

**Step 5: Do not isolate yourself
for too long.**

*Spending some time alone is fine, but
isolation isn't a healthy way to deal with
grief. A friend, a confidant, a spiritual
leader, let someone know. How long were
you in isolation for, how did you break it and
what was that like?*

Gunther:

I lived in isolation for over twenty years. I kept the abuse inside myself because I was afraid to talk about what happened to me until I turned forty years of age. I doubted my perception because I was so young when the abuse began.

I felt powerless when it came to seeking help, I felt ashamed and worried that others would find me repulsive if they knew of what happened to me. I isolated myself emotionally more so than physically from family and friends.

In my case the perpetrator, Scott Williams, was a self-appointed pastor of a Pentecostal church who was well educated, well-liked and well-respected in the community. He achieved effective isolation so powerful by being in such an authoritarian position that it made for a very difficult environment of discovery. Scott Williams leveraged his age, position and role of power.

The exceptional boldness as pastor of a church group was extremely discouraging for me and beyond comprehension. Once I realised that his method of secrecy and protection was highly effective and readily believed I felt totally disempowered.

Scott Williams knew the environment so well which he had set up right from the beginning that he knew, and I felt compelled to protect my family maintaining total and secure secrecy. I kind of sacrificed my health and safety and felt a duty to my family and others around me to protect who were more important to me.

However, that was to change in 2006 when I was informed by a very close friend, (call him Mark), that one of my family members became a victim of Scott Williams sexual assaults. For the first time in over twenty years I have received facts that another person has been sexually abused by Scott Williams. Sadly, it was one of my own family members (one of my nephews - call him Barry). From that time forward, I have shared my story, confronted the perpetrator, and reported him to the police. To break the silence and publicly identify myself was one of the hardest things I have done, but at the same time one of the most freeing experiences I ever have encountered. I am a survivor; I am a victorious survivor and I am stronger for it. I stand triumphantly and move forward, bravely living an abuse free life and helping others to do so too.

Helena:

After the last instance of abuse, I stayed with my partner for another year I think, roughly. But we barely had any sex. Eventually he just moved to a different bedroom. So, I feel that, that was my time of isolation because we were still living in one house, but we were almost like strangers. Living in the same place which was sad but that's what it was. And when I moved out, when I finally broke up with him and moved out, and I had my place for two years, within 2 months I started to invite people over, friends, and I started having a lover.

So, I found it very helpful to start building a community and sort of a tribe and a family around me. And that's the time that I was getting heavily into tantra.

That's when I started doing it, so by going to all these workshops and events, I was building a group of friends who had similar passions and interests. So, it was without a doubt, absolutely such a difference for me to have that community around me who understood and knew what I was going through and where I was sexually.

"And of course, the people that maybe don't have that, there's plenty of services now that, for women especially. Probably not enough for men (although that is changing and there are options for men), but plenty for women to reach out to". -Petros

Helena:

Exactly. But I did seek therapy as well. I saw one sort of standard therapist. But I also saw a tantra practitioner, I saw a shamanic therapist, I saw a spiritual hypnotherapist. I saw a sex coach. I saw several therapists on my pursuit to heal and to get better. Plus, I was building this…

"But you recommend probably not any one particular type of therapy, but you recommend people get therapy where they can and of course find a particular modality(s) that work(s) for them?" -Petros

Helena:

Absolutely. Try different things and you know, first of all do your research online. Whatever you try there but see a number of people, so you know what works for you. Definitely.

Kylie:

I had moments of isolation but never for a great extent. You need a support unit, someone to decompress with, there is no shame but instead courage in asking for help, support, opening up.

Neil:

My good friend and chaplain Bruce is my spiritual guide, the person I can call on for advice with anything. He is a tremendous man, and I am very lucky to have him as a friend and he is a wonderful servant of the lord.

Heather:

What do you mean in isolation?

"So, a lot of people when they go through a trauma they tend to retreat from society and even their families, their friends. They tend to sort of just go away and create their own world where they're just completely alone and isolated so to speak". -Petros

Heather:

I didn't actually do that, I do, or did I guess emotionally cut myself off from people. However, I've always had someone around.

"And how long before you reconnected with those emotions and maybe even express them". -Petros

Heather:

Only a couple probably only about 12 months ago I started fully accepting that I have emotions and feelings like I would get upset and I would cry, and you know like we've had to have a couple of dogs put down and that kind of emotion was there. Things like my husband kissed my best friend in front of me, now most people would get jealous, I didn't feel jealousy I was just like whatever like that kind of thing.

"Is that to say you might feel jealous now that you've sort of reconnected with your emotions".   -Petros

Heather:

I think so when I think about it now I think that I would probably say something because I understand emotions better and it's those kinds of emotions that I keep locked. Otherwise I use anger as a protection like anger has always been my protection, it's always been there and since doing timeline therapy and letting go of anger I don't have that protection anymore. So, when those emotions do come up I don't have the anger there to go I don't care~ *jam it up your clacker~* you know like because it's not there anymore, so I have to deal with the emotions.

I do still find it difficult to deal with those kinds of positive emotions I mean not that jealousy is a positive emotion, but I do still struggle. I don't know......I think I get a bit nervous when I think about it you know because if I let anything too close then you know it can be taken away so to speak.

"And so, you're obviously still working on these things. We're always working on some level, but I guess it's still a bit raw?" -Petros

Heather:

Yeah...... yeah...... well I think so, yeah.

"And would you say it's your gradual acceptance that has helped you to reconnect with emotions or it's made it possible for you to do so?" -Petros

Heather:

Yeah, I think so, like it's just I guess I get the sense that I can't be angry about it because again it's happened you know, and I can't do anything about it like I don't have control of anything that happens around me. I can now or I'm learning to control me. So, anything else that happens is just you got to deal with it there's nothing you can do so you know.

John:

I surrounded myself with people who were going through similar challenges and others who had crossed those bridges regularly in the past. I set aside consumption of all drugs particularly liquor and set about facing my fears rather than attempting to drown them.

In many instances it was a case of two steps forward and one step back but with the passage of time and the support of many people who had given up their drugs and alcohol in a similar fashion I had a roadmap prepared by other people's experiences.

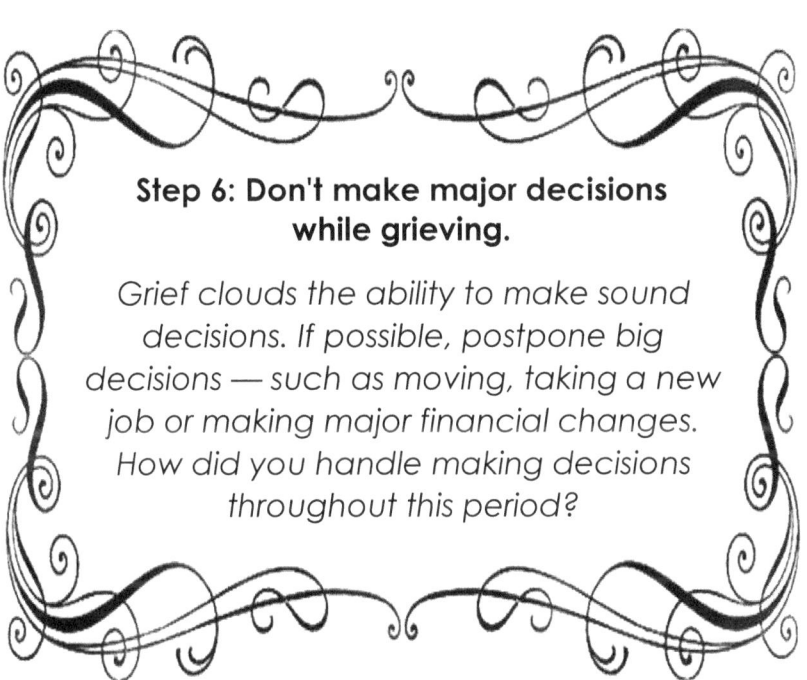

Step 6: Don't make major decisions while grieving.

Grief clouds the ability to make sound decisions. If possible, postpone big decisions — such as moving, taking a new job or making major financial changes. How did you handle making decisions throughout this period?

Gunther:

That probably is wishful thinking. I would agree that one should not make big long-term decisions when grieving. I would highly doubt that anyone who has gone through sexual abuse knows when the time of grieving has started or is finished. As for me, when I told my story and reported the abuse to the police the fun started. There was no time for grieving, there was only time to make decisions, important decisions, to protect my family, who are the most important people in my life, I immediately needed to decide what to do next.

Because of the circumstance where I lived, in Coffs Harbour where the perpetrator was still in power of the church, I believed the best thing to do was to move as far away as possible. I put our house on the market, and I decided to take my family camping around Australia. No job, little saving, but lots of determination.

After a few months of camping we ran out of money in Perth, Western Australia, and I needed to find a job as quickly as possible to put food on the table. As I was working for the church full time for the previous eleven years I needed to educate myself and apply for jobs which I had not done for a long time. I re-educated myself and became a personal trainer, pool Lifeguard, swimming instructor, and pool supervisor within a short period of time.

Probably every circumstance is different to each person, but as for me and my family we needed to make important decisions right there and then. It wasn't easy to make decisions because you are so clouded by what's happened and that's where it can and often does backfire on you, when you are not thinking straight. I did simply because I was under the authoritarian rule of a Scott Williams and his cult for more than half of my life. I was extremely insecure, unsure and indecisive but at the same time determined and excited.

What would be normal for every ordinary person walking the streets, was a new experience to me. During that time my experience with the Australian people was so overwhelming that it is hard to express in words. I am so thankful and grateful to all the wonderful people I have met and made my transition from grief into cheer so much quicker and pleasantly.

Helena:

Life was still forcing me to make decisions. I broke up with someone and I had to move.

"This is more about decisions when people go through a trauma and they become highly emotional, depressed etc... Potentially they become either really reckless or really irrational. It's knowing that a trauma can leave us open to bad decisions. How did you monitor and therefore make your decisions during this time?" -Petros

Helena:

I am really aware of that, the trauma or any sort of negative place can cause us to make bad decisions. So, in that case I always wait. I give myself time. I go and have a cup of tea, or I just postpone, or allow and trust the Universe. In that time, that was my big mantra~ 'I'm trusting the universe.' I don't need to make those decisions right now, I can just allow the universe to take care of things for me. I just knew that being in that bad space mentally; I really couldn't dig myself out of that hole. And really trust the universe that higher force to help me.

"So, what I take from that is to make sure you are giving yourself some time before actually making a decision. Walk away for a bit, come back and see how you feel?" Petros

Helena:

Exactly. That was always very helpful for me.

Kylie:

The only major decision I made was to move, for safety. This was for my own peace of mind. I moved 10 months after the attack. And felt much safer when I did so, everything else, it's wise to take a breath or step away for a small moment during heightened moments of emotion.

Neil:

The decision in the end wasn't difficult but it took some time. It finally came to the conclusion that something had to be done, and the final straw was at my mother's funeral when Gary's mother came up to me and we spoke for a while.

She talked about the past including how Gary used to babysit me. It was just so wrong and awkward. My mother's funeral was hard enough to handle, let alone that as well. That was the defining moment when I started to get clear when I felt able to do so, I decided to take action.

Heather:

Yeah. I think currently the biggest thing Petros is I had 15 years where I was like a slave before I broke away. So, for me so from the age of 10 to the age of 25 I didn't have any decisions to make anyway, you know? Everything was taken out of my control. I did what I was told, everything happened and there was nothing......nothing that I could do.

At 25 I guess the biggest decision was running away. I don't like to call it running away, it's *liberation!* that occurred and after that again for a long time I think because I went into a relationship pretty quickly and that was a controlling relationship as well and I didn't have to make any decisions there. Decisions were made for me and I just did what I was told......again.

"Would you say the decision to get into that relationship that quickly is sort of an example of what we're saying here making a decision whilst you perhaps still clouded in some way whether consciously or subconsciously". - Petros

Heather:

Possibly I think......I think for me at the time it was a protection though; because I'd always been told that he was in the army, he was a sniper, he was like all this stuff and I guess he knew people and he would always come and find me.

He would know where I was, he would always know

where I was no matter where I was, and somebody would find me, and I will either end up dead or back at his place. So, I think for me it was a protection to have somebody there to I guess protect me in a way. So yeah, I think probably making that kind of decision at the time was probably not the correct thing to do and going into a relationship like that was probably not the correct thing to do.

However, for protection at the time because I was still I wasn't the person I am now I was still weak I guess. I wasn't a warrior, so I needed that protection. So that decision was then made.

"You're a warrior now though, aren't you"? -Petros

Heather:

Oh, absolutely!

John:

Screwed that up completely. Was married within a year to a woman that I should not have become married to. We still stuck it out for 14 years and she showed the requisite wisdom by marching out after that time. Word to the wise don't make major decisions while you're still screwed up. If it is more important than "Should I have mayo on my sandwich?" leave it. There will be plenty of time to make carefully and well-informed screw ups later.

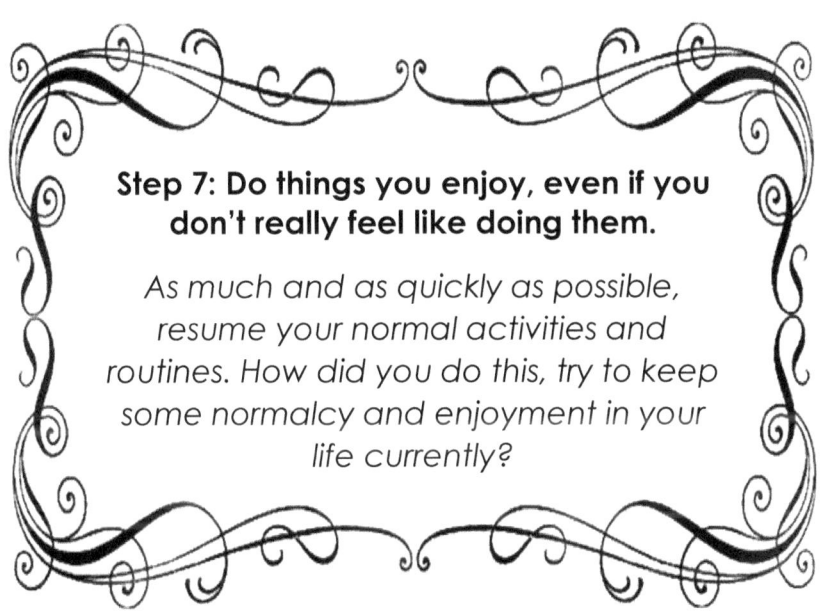

Step 7: Do things you enjoy, even if you don't really feel like doing them.

As much and as quickly as possible, resume your normal activities and routines. How did you do this, try to keep some normalcy and enjoyment in your life currently?

Gunther:

I have touched on this in step number four already. Those things which I really enjoy I have continued doing and added many more enjoyable habits into my life since.

I get a lot of enjoyment through swimming. Being a passionate swimmer since the age of ten I believe healthy exercise gave me physical strength and worked wonders for stress relief. Despite the chlorine, there's a certain feel-good factor that comes from swimming in a pool. In my opinion swimming has therapeutic qualities which aren't limited just to the physical exercise.

I love meditating and spirituality which throughout my years provided me an un-shaken peacefulness. The quietness and silence that one experiences during meditation gets you into a place of disposition free from stress. It is hard to describe but I find my emotional serenity in those moments.

I am a passionate book reader. There is never a time when I do not read a book. Many authors have given me hope, strengths, encouragement, answers and the will to go on, no matter what the situation is. Getting in touch with books that are helpful and useful to read when facing certain problems, believe me can be very therapeutic. I read books to live a better life and to approach any situation more wisely then yesterday.

Meeting new people and making new friends brings many joyful moments into my life. Above all, however, is seeing my children growing up with the truth being told and I do not need to lie any more to anyone. I really enjoy that. Sharing my story, re-educating myself, and learning new things each day, has given me a new perspective of what one can enjoy because I have the freedom to do so......*Then* and now.

Helena:

After over a year of isolating myself, living with my partner and then finally moving out, I just... I felt I had enough, I felt lonely, I needed a family, I needed a tribe and I was single.

Nobody was monitoring anymore, who I was spending time with or who I was going out to have a coffee with and I finally felt free. I'm finally thinking~ *"Ok this is now time to find my tribe and find my group of friends and my joy"*. So, by going to workshops, tantric workshops, that's how I was finding my joy and finding my tribe.

Kylie:

I did this right away, it was a good distraction and way to help me feel normal and eventually start to heal.

Neil:

I like keeping very busy, I am very physical as well in the garden and around the retreat and I train clients in core fitness and balance.

Then on top of that I need to find time for my International Swiss ball performing. I have been performing live since 1999 which has been both enjoyable and challenging. I also have 4 different Swiss ball Guinness World Records to date. I have been eternally grateful for the opportunities to perform on the international stage on some of the world's largest TV shows to more than 500 million TV viewers to date.

I like spending time with my wife. I enjoy travelling the world for performing and holidays. I also like spending time with people who are spiritually uplifting. At the time of my 50th birthday, just after this whole ordeal was finally resolved, I had a small special gathering of people, a wonderful day, my best birthday ever. I even told everyone what had happened, and naturally they were surprised but relieved at the outcome.

It was also at this time when I realised that I have no time anymore for people who are negative, not supportive and especially those with an attitude that suits their own agenda with complete disregard to others.

Heather:

Yeah in my first relationship was when I had my children and it was because of my children that my inner warrior came out. The protection of my children was then my decision. My children then where my life, they were my reason for being, so I guess they were my fun. They're amazing boys so yeah.

So, after that I left, and I was I decided that I would make my own decisions from there, so it was a little while and I discovered horses.

Again, I've been a rider before and then I've had a friend that had a horse and I started riding with her and then I met Paul now and then we got a horse and horses became my thing. So, I always had something to fall back on and that was my happy place. I would go and spend time with my horses when I got too much.

"Animals are great". -Petros

Heather

The best.

"Yeah, they are great to have around while you are healing". -Petros

Heather:

Yeah, they're much more understanding than humans give them credit for.

John:

This is important. During my years of recovery and growth the things that were enjoyable were the things that changed by points of reference. Doing things that I had never done and picking up new challenges.

Early in my recovery I set myself a task. It was largely an academic task, but I thought as I read some materials that it would be an interesting exercise to see if I could reduce the optimal system to live life to one word. At the outset I expected to settle on the word "love", or "empathy" or "peace" or something of that nature. The idea was to then spend years reading anything that I could lay my hands on to inform the search. Religious works, self-help books, (strongly recommend the Road Less Travelled), sales books, fictional novels anything. After about two years and 50 or 60 books I found the word I could settle on.

At the end of that exercise of course it became clear

that the word was nowhere near as important as the journey to get to that point. I loved that journey and it, to this day was a wonderful exercise in living life.

Oh, for the record, the word was "balance".

The other thing that I did was travel. Within six months I was in Africa driving around the country in a clapped-out Toyota Hilux. All of this was about changing points of reference. I did it to break the habits that got me to bad places. By changing the road map, I changed the destinations.

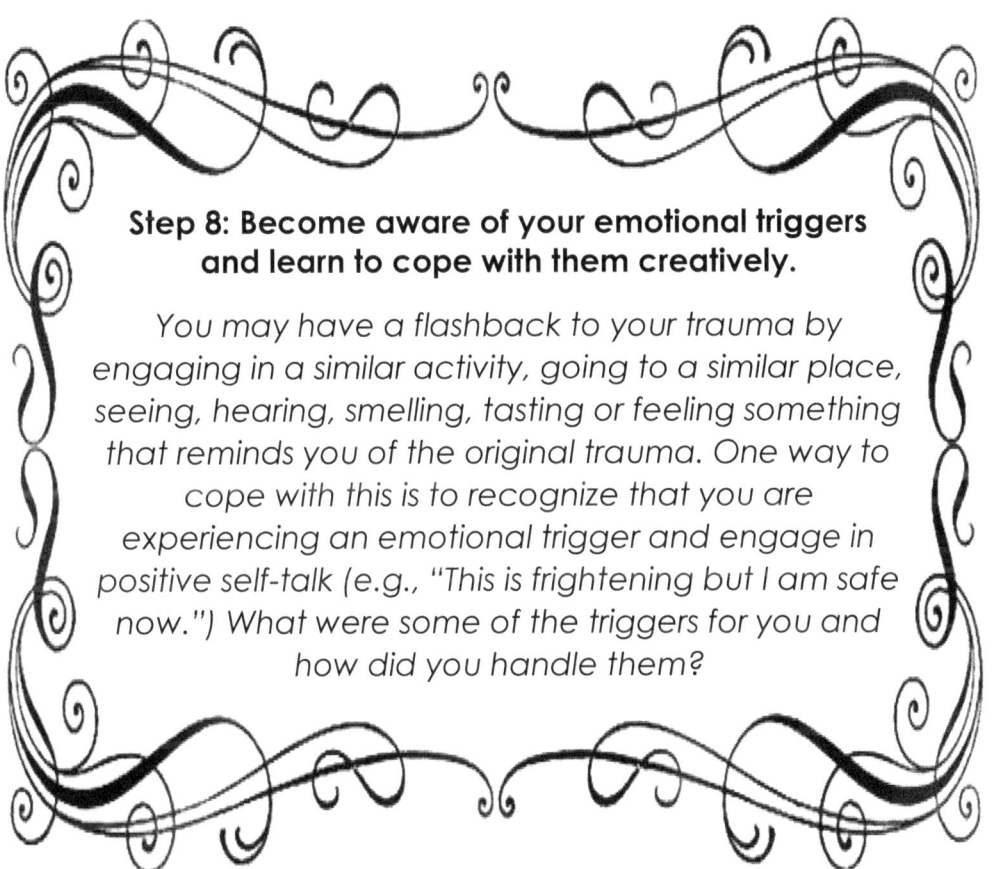

Step 8: Become aware of your emotional triggers and learn to cope with them creatively.

You may have a flashback to your trauma by engaging in a similar activity, going to a similar place, seeing, hearing, smelling, tasting or feeling something that reminds you of the original trauma. One way to cope with this is to recognize that you are experiencing an emotional trigger and engage in positive self-talk (e.g., "This is frightening but I am safe now.") What were some of the triggers for you and how did you handle them?

Gunther:

That's a tough one. My emotional triggers are plentiful and have given me many painful moments throughout my life. To cope with them, probably has been one of the hardest things on my life's journey. No doubt, I've hurt the people I love most, my own family. I have done a lot of things sincerely wrong and can only apologise to all the people I've hurt, foremost my dearest loved ones nearest me.

I was an emotional yo-yo and many situations have triggered my negative emotions to show their ugly head. I despised myself, I hated myself, I had lack of self- esteem, I was depressed, I was angry, I was frustrated, I was fearful, I felt guilty, I felt power-less, and often was not myself for days or weeks on end after I was sexually abused.

My "short-fused temper" even scared me sometimes because it felt like I was not in control of my negative emotions or actions. There are too many triggers in my life to name but living with constant anxiety of, "when will it happen again," has made me a person I am not.

The ability to turn my life around came about on my search to better myself, by reading and attending many kinds of self-development seminars. I came across the neuro-linguistic programming (NLP) courses and techniques which for me became the most effective treatment at that point of time.

By looking after my mind, body and spirit I develop my own inner strengths to improve my life balance and be in control of my attitude and future decisions. Empowering myself to take responsibility for my emotional actions has given me the ability to live the life I always wanted to live.

Helena:

So, men trying to get too close to me too quickly was a trigger. Trying to touch me too quickly is definitely a trigger, and I would just pull away and just give myself time and be gentle with myself when I was triggered like that.

Definitely retreating into my safe space and honouring my need to feel safe.

"And to know that it's ok". -Petros

Helena:

Yeah, exactly. At that stage I already understood that I didn't owe anything to anybody and that I had a full right to protect my body and myself.

"Absolutely, you have every right to your body and to live it however you want it. That's just unfortunate, although not the majority of men It's a shame that still too many men out there think that it's ok to force themselves on a woman". -Petros

Kylie:

I did a lot of deep breaths and told myself I was safe. My triggers were things like his car, his cologne, people that looked like him, places we had been together.

Neil:

The main trigger was the fact that my parents were best friends with Gary's own parents. So, this was always a reminder and trigger of that time in my life. Every time I heard it, I just shut it out and moved on., I was building my power and I trusted in that.

Heather:

Alcohol was probably my major emotional trigger. Once I had had a few drinks I became a different person that's when my emotions started coming out that I had no control of, emotionally unstable I guess, anger; anger was a big one. Anger and hate I had a lot of hate when I was drunk.

"What would trigger anger and the hate? I know you said alcohol is one thing what else, was there any other trigger?" -Petros

Heather:

I don't think so. Generally, it's just alcohol.

"So, you'd go out for dinner or to a mate's you'd have a drink and then bang". -Petros

Heather:

Yeah and probably at the end of the night something I guess maybe something would happen or I don't know and yeah, I don't know what would trigger me at the time and it would just be all of a sudden, I was angry.

"And what did you do then to start managing that and I guess to eliminate it? I'm not sure is it still a trigger for you? if it's not, etc". -Petros

Heather:

Because I'm aware of it now, it doesn't have that hold of me anymore. With my fear, with fear and panic attacks my anxiety I think it was lack of contact, lack of communication so if I rang my husband and he didn't answer his phone then my thoughts would start spinning wildly, you know, *'what if he's had a car accident or truck accident because he drives the truck'*. *'What if he's fallen out of the windmill tower'*, you know, and all those thoughts start milling around.

So, and again it was something that I couldn't control and generally it was lack of contact, lack of being able to get in touch and I would do that even with the children as well. If they ride their bikes to school, then I would worry and panic all day until I was able to pick them up that something had happened to them and nobody had got in touch with me and you know all of that sort of thing.

So, I guess I'm not sure what the actual trigger again would be but I would say lack of contact, lack of communication and even now lack of communication, lack of contact and lack of being able to talk to somebody still gives me that stressed feeling but I'm now able to know it's okay, don't worry about it, where before I would ring my husband like a hundred times a day, *'are you okay?'*

John:

There are rare occasions that there is a trigger. A particular brand of aftershave always transports me back to the sexual assaults and the smell of beer also transports me back decades to a much less settled time.

Oddly, however, after a while I sought out triggers as my equilibrium was established. The spectres which tormented me so awfully were held up to the light and viewed through the lens of a new perspective. Each time I embraced them those ghouls became increasingly small. Demons that haunted my consciousness became no more significant than Casper.

Fears still visit me and there are still times of mild depression, but my approach has become a system by which I embrace rather than resist them. If a fear occupies my mind I look at it and analyse it. It is examined and measured so that its magnitude can be determined. Through that process I still deal with whatever issue is presented to me in the form of that fear and from time to time there are good grounds to be frightened. But I have not yet had a fear which has killed me, so the survival rate has been a source of more than a little reassurance.

In the last year of my drinking the emotional swings were awful. Several hours of the absolute certainty that I could conquer the world and then a calamitous crash to the bottom of a slimy dark crevasse that suffocated me and struggling for breath. Removing the chemicals certainly helped with my recovery but also a new mindset. I have always had times, even today, where I am visited by the darkness. Many people who I have known with a similar visitor resist that with a "fake it till you make it" optimism which when I tried to take that approach struck me as forced and not self-honest.

Instead, I have chosen to allow the visitor to visit. Churchill's black dog. I know when it's there. But rather than resist I simply invite it in. Offer it a chair in the metaphorical lounge room of my soul and accept that it's there. This is when I decide to be mellow. I accept its presence and I just drop back a cog. That's a time to do mellow things. Swim at the beach, walk in a botanical garden and do sensual things like turn my face to the sun and feel its warmth.

It stays for a while and for a lack of better terms it seems to be bored after a few days and it leaves. Bizarrely, it has become manageable through surrender. To this day I accept the visitor and the jagged lines of my ups and downs which look like a stock market graph have become the gentle undulations of English fields. The downs, through that mechanism for me, whilst not enjoyed lead to behaviour that I do enjoy.

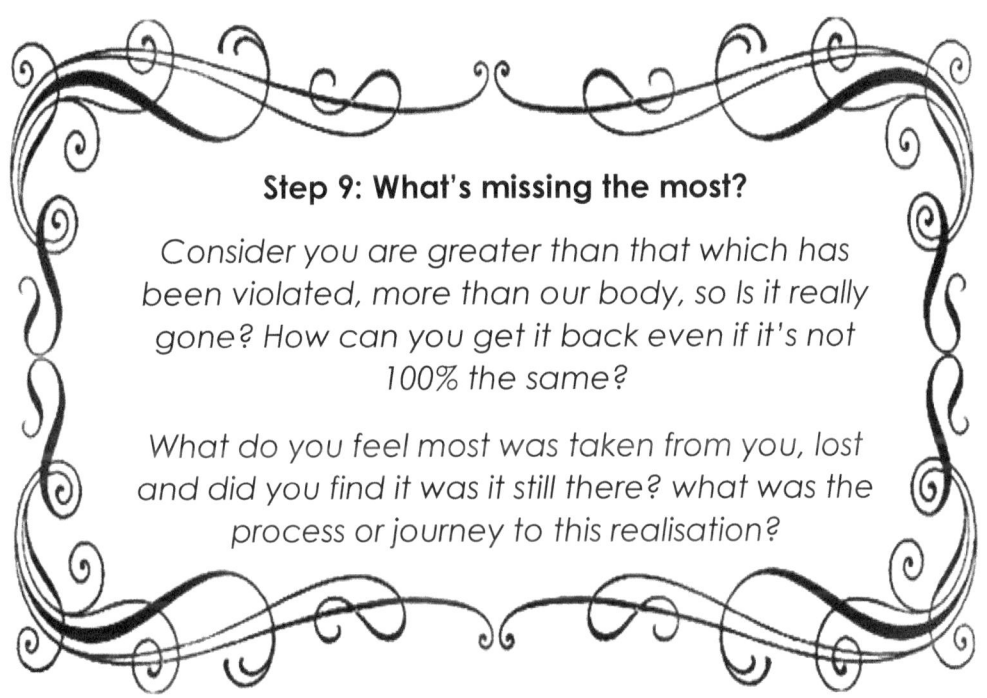

Step 9: What's missing the most?

Consider you are greater than that which has been violated, more than our body, so Is it really gone? How can you get it back even if it's not 100% the same?

What do you feel most was taken from you, lost and did you find it was it still there? what was the process or journey to this realisation?

Gunther:

Every wound creates pain and it takes time for it to heal and heal it will if you let it. Yet a scar will always be present. I am aware now, that I am greater than the abuse or violation on my life, but what has been taken from me can never be retrieved.

As I mentioned before, I believe when you are abused as a child, whether you know it or not, your innocence is stolen away from you. A piece of your childhood is gone. The innocence that I felt entitled to have, is no longer mine to have. I guess, it is only natural that one would feel the loss from that forever.

Being sexually abused as a child is feeling a kind of loss of "what could have been". Often in my life I wonder what kind of person I might have been if I had never been abused! I certainly would not have some of the anxious behaviours that I do now!

Saying that, however, I believe that I have found so many more important and valuable Life lessons because of my past. I'm not able to change the past, who is? Yet on my life journey I have been privileged to gain insights and learnings which I may have never experienced if it wasn't for the violations.

Let me quote from one of my heroes, Viktor E. Frankle, who said: *"It can be said that they were worthy of their sufferings; the way they bore their suffering was a genuine inner achievement. It is in this spiritual freedom - which cannot be taken away - that makes life meaningful and purposeful."* (Man's Search for Meaning by V. E. Frankle).

Helena:

I'm really missing; well what I've been missing for so many years was a connection with my body. And a deep love and appreciation of what it means to be a woman and have this body full of sensuality, juice, joy and emotions and being able to honour that and follow that. Follow my pleasure as being a woman.

When I hear about other women that didn't have such traumatic experiences and that they from a very young age were discovering self-touch and self-pleasuring and playing with their bodies, and slowly, naturally discovering that juiciness and that sensuality of their bodies.

I never had that, from my very early sexual experiences. It was pain and trauma, so I was withdrawing from my body, I was disconnecting from my body. I was living in my head, because my body was not a safe or not a pleasurable place.

"Was there something specific that the traumas took away from you? Something perhaps you were able to get back a sense of innocence maybe or even your sense of power. Because, the reason why I'm asking further is; I acknowledge what you said about the disconnect of your body, but that kind of begun from your upbringing. You didn't lose it because of the rapes". -Petros

Helena:

Faith in men. Yeah. And the ability to trust men and to feel safe around men.

"Did you get that back, or is that still a work in progress?"
-Petros

Helena:

I got that back.

"How?" -Petros

Helena:

By changing who I attract into my life. And by attracting beautiful, loving, caring men who were prepared and ready to show me again, and again, and again that I could trust them. And that they wouldn't hurt me. Even when I felt triggers or discomfort at the beginning of relating, each time they would show me that I am safe.

They would not push me, not abuse me, they would not use my body.

"And it also sounds like you recognised that you had the power and the choice for that to happen, amazingly". -Petros

Helena:

Oh my god, absolutely! I've realised I've claimed back that power to my body and to my sensuality and to protect myself in relationships with men. And acknowledge that I am a perfectly valid human being.

Kylie:

My confidence and trust were taken the most. It felt like I had been brought down to nothing and wasn't able to trust any men again. It's something that happened instantly to me, I knew right away these were gone. I remember answering the door late one night with '000' ready on my phone in one hand and a knife in the other. That's when I knew I had to stop and *get help* and reclaim that trust and faith.

Neil:

I wanted respect and my dignity restored. I needed Gary to acknowledge that I am a human being with a life of my own and how I felt. I let him know that he has avoided this issue and without really thinking about how I may have felt about it over all the years. Initially, I was a bit angry with him in our first communication, including asking him things like "How would you feel if this happened to one of your children?"

Gary himself was violated, which certainly would have helped him to understand. I am more than satisfied with the outcome.

Heather:

I guess the only thing I feel that I lost is my childhood because, I mean right up until the age of 10 I was a child but from the age of 10 I was no longer allowed to be a child.

So, all those little girl things that you get to do and your first love and... *(Begins to tear up)* Sorry...... Yeah just that kind of thing.

"Yeah no worries that's plenty" -Petros

John:

There is no possibility after any challenge of this nature to return anywhere. Personally, there was nothing that I sought to return to. There was little in my past that I particularly wanted to preserve. In truth even if there was something that I wanted back, the reality of all that occurred could not recover an innocence lost.

When something like innocence is corrupted then it is gone. That is the nature of experience.

For me what I sought was for something noble that could be carved from the rocks of the avalanche of destruction. This for me is better than harking to some point of innocence lost because it is stronger.

Innocence's antithesis is corruption, but the antithesis of corruption isn't innocence, it is nobility, it is correctness. Nobility and ethical conduct can stand in the presence of corruption and be unaffected by them. Innocence cannot defend itself against corruption. Innocence has no tools to resist corruption. The moment innocence can challenge corruption it could logically no longer be called innocence.

For that reason, I have never sought it. What I have sought is a code of personal conduct that places correctness and ethical conduct in the forefront of my thinking.

The second component is to accept that this is a spiritual/ethical goal to work towards and not an absolute.

Striving for correctness is the goal. Absolute correctness, well I'll leave that for people who walk across swimming pools.

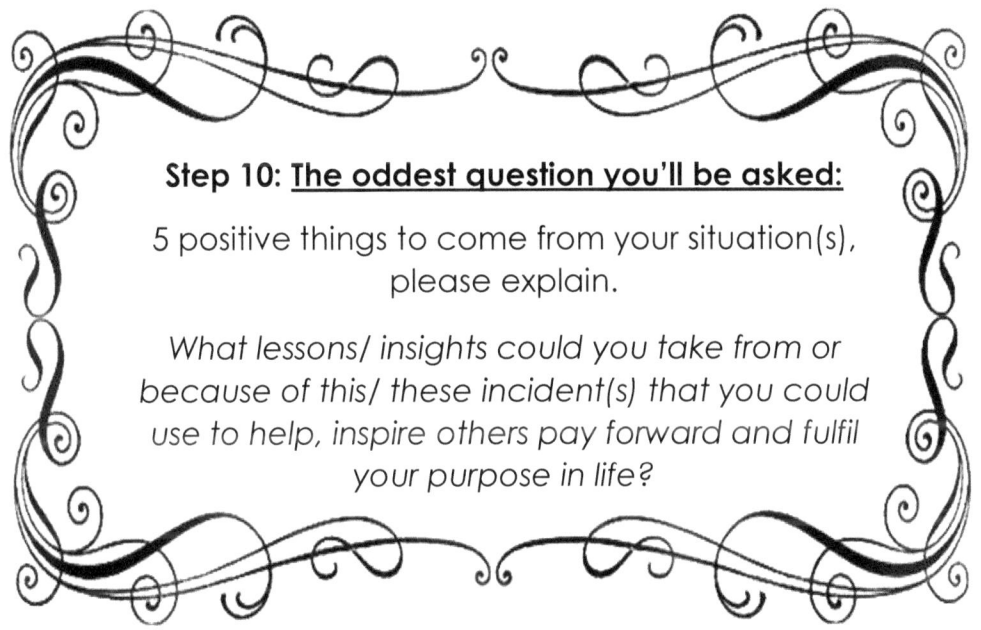

Step 10: <u>The oddest question you'll be asked:</u>

5 positive things to come from your situation(s), please explain.

What lessons/ insights could you take from or because of this/ these incident(s) that you could use to help, inspire others pay forward and fulfil your purpose in life?

Gunther:

5 Positive Things I have learned:

1. I learned to believe in myself.

2. I learned to know that I am okay.

3. I learned that the sexual abuse is something that had happened to me, but it does not define who I am.

4. I learned that recovery is a process.

5. I learned that I am a survivor.

Helena:

First, what I already mentioned is the compassion, to other women or other people in general and understanding what they are going through, what they have gone through. Because I have been there myself.

"Certainly!"-Petros

Helena:

Also, a big kick up my butt to educate myself about sex, so that was a huge inspiration to learn about good sex and beyond great sex, sacred sex. Tantra was a huge gift and a huge positive thing that came out of that situation. Because Tantra changed my life around. When I discovered Tantra it was the first day of the rest of my life.

"I do relate, and I actually do want to do a bit of work with Tantra around that sexual healing myself. Not necessarily professionally but I can certainly relate to the effectiveness of it. Number 3?" -Petros

Helena:

Deeper understanding of men and masculine nature.

"Good for you. This is very inspiring. Number 4?" -Petros

Helena:

Um. I guess the opportunity to see my victim. And to heal that victim side of me. My tendency to be a victim.

"That's powerful. I can't even speak, Number 5?" -Petros

Helena:

Ok, so what's coming to me now is this wounded healer emotion. It was like a rite of passage. It was a sort of ceremony of fire to prepare me to do the kind of work, of sexual healing I do with other people. It was like, my real rite of passage!

Kylie:

- Find a place you can turn off and re-energise and process, that you can begin to relax in.

- Seek beauty in the world around you and with tough times practice perspective and seeking the guidance and wisdom.

- Look for the good things around you.

- Practice gratitude.

- Do something you love,.

Neil:

1. The development of mutual resolve.

2. The incredible strength and love through forgiveness.

3. The courage to do it.

4. A closer bond between myself and my good chaplain friend, Bruce.

5. That I am actually friends with Gary. In fact, the length of communication is sometimes longer than my closest friends.

Heather:

1. I am stronger than what I thought. I can go through a lot and I can deal with a lot and I can understand people so much better because of what happened to me.

2. You can start to heal whenever you want, sooner than you think, so work on self always and build coping skills.

3. Remove judgment.

4. Be open is another thing, you know if you can even give a little bit of your story and help one person with that; isn't that better than not helping anyone? So be open.

5. Be happy there's nothing, nothing can happen to you in this world that you can't overcome and if you can smile and be happy then the effects of that person or that thing that happened to you no longer has any control over you.

John:

Fredrich Nietzsche's philosophy gave us the understanding that what doesn't kill you makes you stronger. There is truth in that. The risk of trying to forge something in a furnace however is that you can also break it. This is the challenge that we as people who are going to such a place face. Often what happens can end in a cell, in a psych ward or even a grave. Many do.

But having made that observation, there is little that life has been able to throw at me that has been able to gravely hurt me since. I used to describe it as a suit of armour, but that analogy is wrong. Armour can be breached. What I have learned from my experiences has not resisted the slings and arrows but rather allowed them to pass through without doing any damage. There seems, at an emotional level at least to be a difference between the concept of resistant and impervious.

In the film the Matrix there is a heavy reliance on the works of a French postmodern philosopher Jean Baudrillard entitled Simulacra and Simulation. Without entering into the work too much the thrust is that we have surrounded ourselves with affections that merely represent reality, but they are not reality itself. This is the core of the film. But at the end of the film the anti-hero, Neo, is shot at by the guardians of the matrix. Because Neo can see the matrix for what it is at an instinctive level he stops the bullets and they fall harmlessly to the floor.

This isn't correct if the work is to be understood. The better interpretation would have been to allow bullets to pass through Neo leaving him untouched. The bullets that we see as a danger aren't real. They don't matter, they have no consequence. That would have suited the message of the philosopher better and that is how I now perceive those dangers that I once thought so real. I'm not at all resistant to those things, merely impervious.

So, what are the positives?

1. My ability to give of myself to others. My wife, my children my community.

2. To act with integrity and to honestly self-appraise my own motives. Okay that's a stretch as this is hard to achieve but at least the tool is in the toolbox.

3. To be reliable.

4. To stand up and be counted for what is important and right. This includes in the physical sense. I have intervened on several occasions in stopping violence, particularly against women. On one occasion that earned me a bloodied nose but rather a few moments of pain rather than a life time of knowing I had turned away.

5. To have a personal philosophy with values and value.

I don't know if I would have developed these traits or not in my life had I not faced the challenges that I had. But I can trace each of those lessons directly to my experiences as a rejection of the corruption in which I had been immersed. If I had developed those values by another mechanism I would guess that they would have still required a trauma of some form to give them the meaning I ascribe to them today.

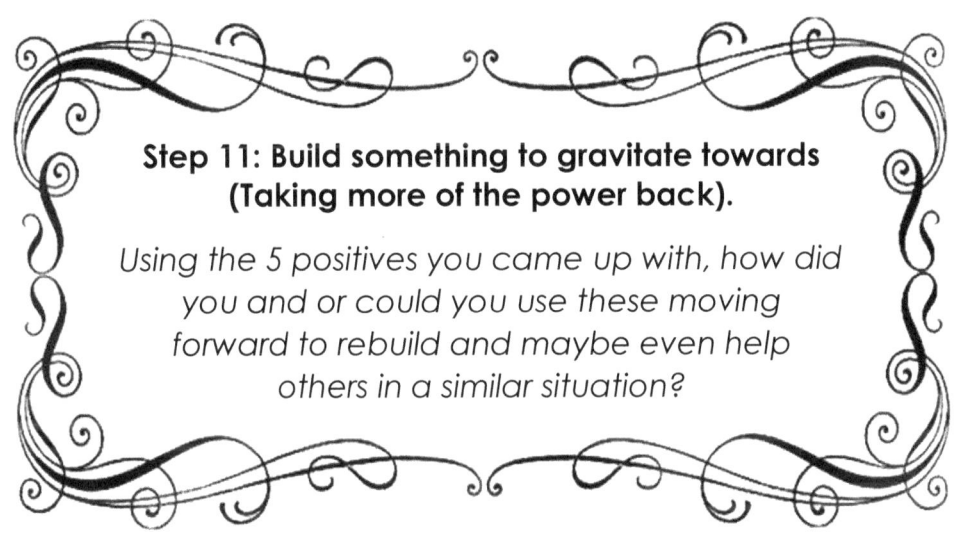

Step 11: Build something to gravitate towards (Taking more of the power back).

Using the 5 positives you came up with, how did you and or could you use these moving forward to rebuild and maybe even help others in a similar situation?

Gunther:

1. I learned to believe in myself.

That maybe sounds strange to many, but I had to learn to believe in myself as a grown-up adult after those many years of trauma. I had very little self-esteem and self-belief that I doubted myself all the time. Now, I am doubting my doubts. I have learnt to talk to myself and believe in myself everyday now.

2. I learned to know that I am okay.

Deep down no matter what, I know I'm okay. Nothing will change that unless I let someone else 'drive my car' again and that's not okay. I'm okay with every situation, in every situation and for every situation because all situations are okay. It is just a matter of how I approach the situation and my approach is okay because it is mine. I take responsibility for my response therefore I own it.

3. I learned that the sexual abuse is something that had happened to me, but it does not define of who I am.

I can be anyone I want to be, my past situation does not define my future. I am who I am because of the decisions I make, right now, in this moment. I may not be able to control the circumstance, but I can always control my attitude towards the circumstance. The past is gone, the future is mine.

4. I learned that recovery is a process.

I live by the motto; "Stop learning, stop growing!" Patience is a virtue, how true! I believe that we're on the journey and each day we turn a page in our book of life.

And one day, on the last page, it will say; "The End" but until then it is a process of learning, relearning, and unlearning all the things we have been taught. All is within and we, ourselves need to retrieve it - whatever it is for each individual.

5. I learned that I am a survivor.

Through personal development courses over the last decade, I have been able to change my world around. I am a sexual abuse survivor. I can tell you what the abuse felt like for me and what kind of healing process got me to where I am today. Therefore, my goal is to spread awareness of the nightmares victims of sexual abuse encounter.

I have dedicated my life to seeking remedy and resolve for victims of sexual abuse. My story represents hope for the hopeless. I want to help others see that it is worthwhile to tell their story and find liberty and freedom with the knowledge a person should never feel shame or guilt because of others' wrong doing. I am a survivor!

Helena:

Those 5 positives definitely propelled me forward into who I am right now, who I am professionally. And how I serve my clients. Definitely.

"So, the positive that you created to move towards was this sense of this professional self and your human self, but also, you've brought that into your practice as well. So, you built your practice based around who you've become professionally and non-professionally from the 5 things of your experiences?" -Petros

Helena:

Exactly. I definitely use all these 5 positive things to build the life that I am living now, and I am extremely passionate about it. It brings me a lot of joy and it brings my clients a lot of value.

Because I don't just speak about things I learnt in books. I speak about real life experience that I had myself, and I guided a lot of clients through as well.

So, my experiences were sort of a shamanic initiation in a way, to helping others and healing others on their path.

Kylie:

Find a place you can turn off, you do feel safe, that you can begin to relax in. For me this was nature. I would sit for hours next to a waterfall and just simply stare at the beauty in the world around me.

Look for the good things around you. Each day find something to be grateful for and look at things from different perspectives and go with what positively serves you.

Do something you love, I love soccer and I joined my old soccer team and started playing again and I felt *FREE and HAPPY!*

Neil:

I have been thinking whether to offer my services to other victims of abuse in conjunction with my health and fitness coaching as a specialty and a way of spreading the good I have drawn from my experience.

I want to keep in contact with Gary and remain good friends. It beats having hate and, in my case, this works well.

Heather:

Okay so basically overcoming, you must change your focus that's probably the biggest thing; people tend to focus on one thing and when you're focusing on that one thing then that controls all your thoughts and it takes over everything. So, I guess everybody's obsessive in one way or another so take control, be aware of what's happening, be aware of what's around.

I did hypnosis, NLP timeline therapy, with these you can let go of the past and that's probably my biggest I guess gripe with things is, you read everywhere and people say all the time you know that you can't just let it go, you can't leave it behind you, we know it's in the past it still affects my future and that's all decisions that you've made.

So, I guess to let go of that you need to accept that you can actually let it go and leave it behind. You can leave it all in the past. It doesn't have to come forward into your future with you every step of the way because it happened, you can't change it, let it go and move forward, draw the wisdom and move on.

"So just to sort of connect it a little bit better, how did you come across for example hypnosis, was that something you took as a modality to help you get through your situation? "-Petros

Heather:

I think I needed to help people. I discovered with hypnotherapy, initially I did it. I did the course to help people quit smoking and all of that I was looking for something for me to do and go through. From that I discovered other things that you could do with hypnosis and I realized then that you can help people, or I can help people.

So, using hypnosis for me was a natural step and I guess my drive to help people that have been not necessarily just through what I've been through but through any kind of traumatic event. If you can understand what you went through then that leads to a better learning and leads you to be able to let it go, because it happened and good things happen to bad people and bad things happen to good people, but good things happen to good people and bad things happen to bad people.

"There's a lot of wisdom there. So, it's therefore important to at some stage, make the decision that you're going to give something to yourself, a positive for yourself to move towards. Would you agree with that comment?" -Petros

Heather:

Absolutely, you've got to give yourself a reason to want to move forward.

There's so many people I know and even after I've spoken to them they don't have that thing, that's what they focus on and they don't have that you know you've got to have something and that's your path that's your life goal, that's where you're going to end up and your path goes like this it's not straight.

We'd all love for the path to go from here to here everything's great and everything's smooth and nothing goes wrong but it's not. The path is wide and very narrow and up and down and you know sharp and soft and smooth and you have to accept that path and work through that path, but you've got to have that one thing that is leading you to where you need to go. And that's the hardest thing to get through to people is that one thing that takes your past what you've been through and into what you can do and be.

John:

Part of all of what I have been through has placed a responsibility upon me. I have received a gift, perhaps by a divine hand or perhaps by a mechanism of the human condition but whatever the source of the gift, to retain it, I paradoxically must give it freely to others. Stand ready to connect and share of what you gain. It is not a commodity. It grows. As you sow it you will reap its rewards. The more generously given the more bountiful it becomes.

Given a reasonably unique experience there will be others who will benefit from it. They deserve peace as you have been granted peace. At the risk of going a little Christian in this space, love one another, is a pretty good notion.

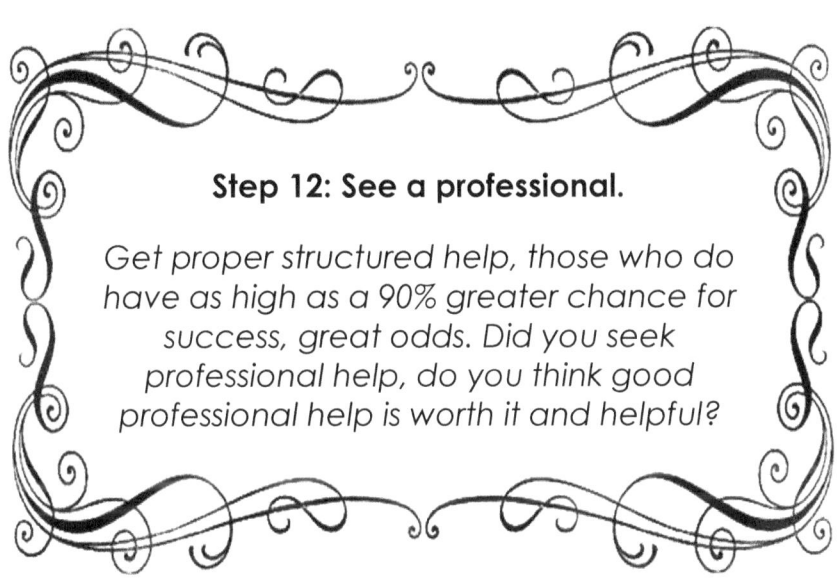

Step 12: See a professional.

Get proper structured help, those who do have as high as a 90% greater chance for success, great odds. Did you seek professional help, do you think good professional help is worth it and helpful?

Gunther:

Yes, I did and yes, you should too. I found it very challenging to cope with my intense negative emotions which plagued me for a long time during and after my abuse. I struggled to find peace and happiness in my life, because distressing memories, anxiety, and trust issues were blocking me.

To unblock your stuck state of mind you need to find a way to free it. To achieve this, I received help from several counsellors and psychotherapy over a long period of time. Those qualified mental-health professionals have given me the opportunity to simply empty myself by listening. To discuss my abuse openly without being judged was an incredibly good feeling. They were like a sounding board and that alone allowed me to recover new positive thoughts into my life.

At the same time, I searched for additional self-help books, material, went to seminars, and workshops which worked best for me. We are all individuals who are from different backgrounds, that is, family, culture, religion, country - all of us are unalike and there is not one formula which works for everyone.

Great changes occurred for me when I started to connect with myself through Neuro-Linguistic Programming (NLP), meditation and spirituality. This path not only made a huge difference in my life, but it also revealed why we, as human beings, hang onto our false beliefs, limited decisions and thought processes. I believe if one way doesn't work – there is always another way. Never give up. By looking at different concepts and strategies it is easier to figure out how things can work for you as they did for me.

Helena:

There are no ifs or buts about it, professional help, the right one for you is an important and integral part of your journey and healing, explore and seek what and more importantly who works for you.

Kylie:

Don't be ashamed to ask for help. I saw two counsellors, one was a friend and one was unbiased, and both helped me immensely. Even if it is as simple as getting techniques to calm your anxiety it is well worth it.

Neil:

On my planned Day of Reconciliation, I organised a psychologist and an entrusted Chaplain and special friend in Bruce, for Gary and me to attend together. For us, it was the key to success. I think one needs to be organised and prepared. My idea was to have a psychologist to meet the needs of confronting the past, to take responsibility and to learn about respecting the other person. The role of Bruce was to confront God and to reveal oneself with all their glory, have no shame, but to move on to the next journey of life, and to seek forgiveness. Very powerful. For this, I love Bruce very much.

I feel support is essential. Perhaps people have the right family members to call on, or perhaps it is not best to involve family, and to seek private support. Everyone's experience will be different requiring their own unique way in which to resolve. Rest assured though, all can be healed with your spiritual self in-tact, ready to surge forth in life once again. I wish all those my best.

Heather:

It is very important for someone to seek professional help initially yes. For me it was a merry-go-round. Go and see the doctor, go and see the psychiatrist, go and see the psychologist, go and see the counsellor, tell your story, tell everything, do this, do that, take this drug. And it's a cycle and you go through it and then that drug stops working and they put you on another one and that drug keeps you awake at night so they put you on that one to help you sleep and then that drug has other side effects that you need and you go through this cycle until you get to where your doctor says well I think what you need to do is go on this drug that's psychiatrist prescribed and you go **NO!**

I don't want to do that anymore. So, it is very important that you seek help initially and that the drugs aren't bad they can help kick-start your brain, but you also need to be aware that that's all they know. It's the biggest needs to me. All they can do is give you more drugs so take the initiative and take the step yourself as well. Do some research, do your own research, work out what works for you and who works for you, explore, understand that.

Things like nutrition have a huge impact on your body, on the way you're feeling, on the things that you do, even the chemicals in your brain are dictated by what you put into your body. Be aware of all of that you know and understand that you don't have to resort to drugs like there are other things that you can do.

Exercise again releases endorphins in your body, the feel-good emotions come from that.

Absolutely seek help but understand that you know your body better than anyone else. Allow yourself that understanding and learn for yourself what and who works for you.

John:

Professionals are so necessary in breaking the mindsets that have become the prison. Get help from both the trained and the experienced and remember they are often not the same person.

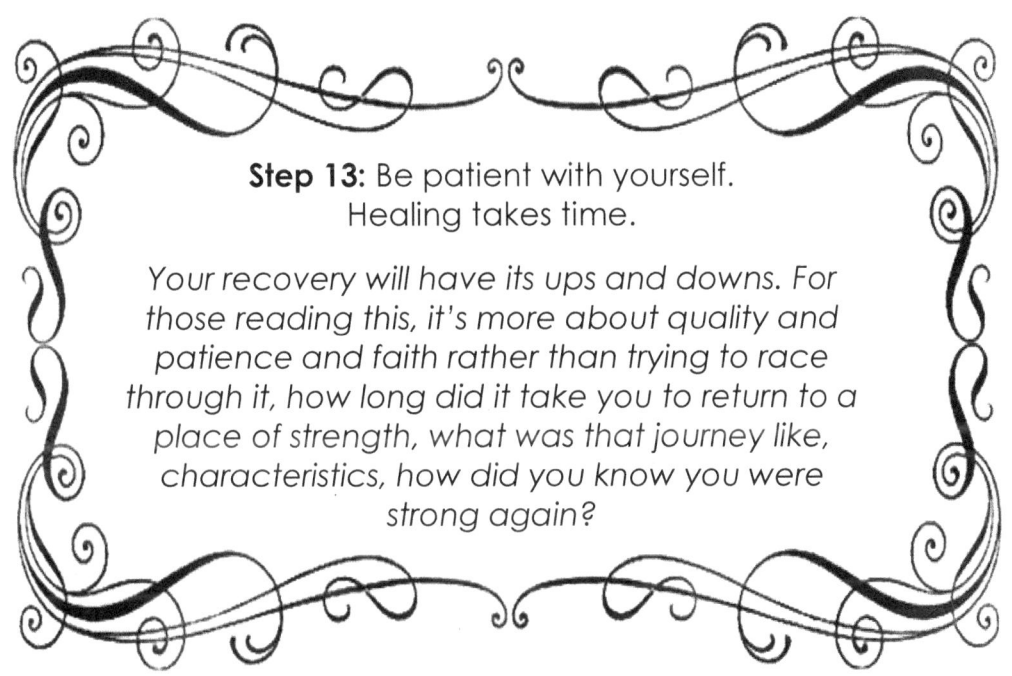

Step 13: Be patient with yourself.
Healing takes time.

Your recovery will have its ups and downs. For those reading this, it's more about quality and patience and faith rather than trying to race through it, how long did it take you to return to a place of strength, what was that journey like, characteristics, how did you know you were strong again?

Gunther:

Patience is a virtue. What does this really mean? Opinions may differ here, but I don't think that patience is a virtue. Some use a similar phrase; "good things come to those who wait." I am sure we all have had experiences that good things never come to those who wait. Perhaps the ability to wait for something without getting angry or upset is a valuable lesson and quality to learn and possess. Healing takes time, yes that is true, but it is a daily process to look after your wounds towards perfect recovery.

I think that recovering from a sexual abuse is a process, and that process looks different for everyone. It may take weeks, months, years, and in some cases never..., there's no timetable for healing. Definitely it took me the best part of five years to feel absolute re-aligned within myself. I found my journey of self-discovery a little mixed with different feelings. One of excitement and sometimes even a little scary, but overall, full of enjoyment and happiness.

Though I am not kidding myself, my journey will only be complete when I take my last breath on planet earth.

Helena:

The full journey for me to get to a place where I was really good, and I felt like I had done my healing, sex feels amazing and I am empowered, I am in control of my sexuality- that was 2 years.

"2 years, ok. And how did you know you arrived? How did you know you were there?" -Petros

Helena:

Because everything was different. Because sex felt very, completely different for me. Because finally, there was no more tears, no more pain, no more frustration, no more discomfort during sex.

I felt, sex had become an amazing and beautiful experience and union between me and my partner. So, take the time your journey requires, we never stop really evolving anyway, it's how we do it.

Kylie:

The journey was very much up and down. At the start it was hard, nightmares were regular and then they slowly became weekly, fortnightly, monthly. The triggers were just as bad, but they begin to settle too with time. I never tried to rush myself with these things.

It took me about 14 months to get to a point where I felt strong again, were I thought I had a real chance of being me again. I felt more like me with time and it would have been about 18months later where it really began to feel like me.

Feeling like me again was the most amazing thing, that moment in time when your conscious goes... oh hey you, your back. Is that a real smile on your face? Is the moment you know it will be okay and you've reached the moment in your life that things will once again go your way.

Neil:

It's not a race, it's about exploration, discovery, even a coming of age, take your time, don't force it or resist it, allow it to unfold and be present to it and its lessons, it's about healing yourself and re-uniting with yourself.

Heather:

How did I know I was strong enough? I don't know how I knew, I just knew. I just knew that...

"Was it a feeling or was it a thought"-Petros

Heather:

No, I think it's a feeling just knowing in my heart more than anything else because my head still spins sometimes but, in my heart, in my body I know that I'm strong enough that I'm more than capable and that anything that gets thrown at us is for a purpose.

You don't need to know what the purpose is, face the challenge overcome it and you'll learn. You'll know, you'll understand whatever it is you need to understand, and the understanding comes from allowing things, not allowing things to happen to you, allowing yourself that process of learning and evolving.

John:

Change will come, and the pain will ease. Change comes but sometimes imperceptibly. Take your time and forgive yourself. Peace is there to be had.

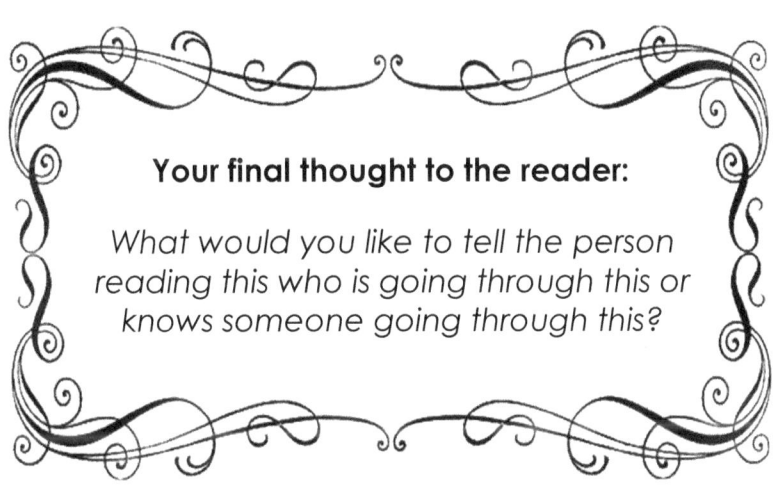

Your final thought to the reader:

What would you like to tell the person reading this who is going through this or knows someone going through this?

GIFT 1: FREE FOR YOU ONLINE PROGRAM:

4 Fun Steps To Overcoming The Doldrums.

We all hit a plateau in our life, connect with your creative and authentic self and in 4 fun steps create, map out and action the next phase of your life. Be it a full major new chapter or just a minor direction adjustment.

Plus

GIFT 2: FREE ACCESS-MASIVELY IMPROVE YOUR MINDSET IN 30 DAYS:

30 Day Beat The Blues Challenge.

Do it on your own, with a friend or in a group, even at work. The 30 Day Beat The Blues Challenge is designed for you to take on simple but highly effective and specifically chosen tasks over a 30 day period. The sole purpose and aim of this challenge is to help you improve your mindset, for with an improved mindset comes improved outlook, improved decision making and therefore improved outcomes. You to can be manifesting greater results for you 30 days from now, start today.

Go to: www.yougotthismentalhealth.com.au/bonuses

GIFT 3: 2 COMPLIMENTARY TICKETS

Events by Petros (You Got This: Mental Health Services) are informative, empowering, practical and relevant.

You and a friend are invited to a non-workshop event and its Petros' shout.

With topics such as:

- Beating Panic Brain
- 3 Common things you do normally that you shouldn't do when having experienced a crisis or trauma
- 7 Steps to overcoming a crisis faster and better.

Use coupon code: RFTLBOOK on an eligible event you want to see. To be notified of upcoming events register through below link:

Go to: www.yougotthismentalhealth.com.au/events

Gunther:

It's not always easy to know what to say when someone tells you they've been sexually assaulted, especially if they are a friend or family member.

For a survivor, disclosing to someone they care about can be very difficult, so I would encourage to be as supportive and non-judgmental as possible.

I would never pretend to them *"you know how they feel!"* I would never presume what it was like for them!

Most importantly I would say that listening is the best way to support a survivor. In some cases, you may assist in providing resources to seek out qualified mental health professionals or report the crime to the police.

If you are a survivor, I'll encourage you to each day take small steps of action because you are NOT alone. There is help and support which will guide you through your hardship to victorious freedom which you deserve.

I am not saying it is easy, but it is worth it, and you are worth it - absolutely. You are not alone! It might be extremely difficult to come forward and share your story (and I do not mean publicly). You may feel ashamed, concerned, worried or doubt that it really happened. All those emotions you feel are entirely normal and let me assure you, it is not your fault. I would love to see you pursuing liberty and freedom and become who you really are - yourself. You are a survivor! You have already done the hardest part; you survived the sexual abuse. You are much stronger and bigger than you think you are!

Helena:

You're not broken. It's not your fault. What you experienced was painful and you have a full right to grieve and to cry. But moving on will take you beyond anything that you ever thought possible. And the world of healing and transformation is powerful, you can achieve anything you want.

Kylie:

The enemy does not stand a chance when the victim decides to survive

In the weeks to follow the attack and to this day I am open about what happened to me, not for the 'poor you' card or 'you're so brave' card but for those who have suffered, male or female and for those 'it will never happen to'. Be aware that it's okay to talk about it, to cope the way you need to and for those that it will never happen to, it can happen to anyone. I thought I would never be subjected to such a crime. I stood up and pressed charges (defamation of liberty, assault causing bodily harm, sexual assault and stealing) despite the lengthy process that it is, we awaited 22 months for a date for trial. Still, hopefully by standing up to this bully he will never hurt another woman.

I wouldn't change the event for the relationships and strength I have found along the way for it is a true gift, yes, I missed parts of the old me that aren't brave enough to shine just at those times you knew they usually would, but they will once more, given time. So here is a toast to the men and women who have fought and won against violence and to those currently in the situation or dealing with it, I send you the biggest hug for the nights you need it the most, a smile when you see no good in the world around you, a kind word when your too hard on yourself, a calm place to retreat to when your anxiety is triggered, and a hand when you feel like you can't face the day.

Those currently torn and broken through domestic violence, please don't think for a second it was easy, it's not, and I know I don't have to tell you that, but I will tell you this.... YOU CAN, and YOU WILL be the person you were before, just a little wiser and a little more cautious and that's okay. Make sure you ask for help, cry when you need, scream when you need to, laugh when it feels impossible to do so, be honest to yourself and those around you.

Be strong, be vulnerable, be courageous. **BE YOU**.

To those battling the situation and the aftermath, keep fighting, take a breath, take time for you to clear your mind and steady your soul, stay safe, and be patient with the process, you can survive, and you will survive.

To the friends and family, stay close, stay strong, stay open and most importantly let your loved one know they are loved, and you can see them and their struggle. You may not understand it and that's okay, simply being there is what we need.

I want to thank all my friends and family thank you for your support, I know I was lost for a bit and many of you were worried if I would return to my old bubbly self. I am so happy to say I am almost the woman I was beforehand just smarter and stronger.

I want to thank everyone who stood by me, wiped my tears, held my hand, gave me a place to stay when I was too scared to stay at home, made me laugh, let me vent and deal with it in my own way, without you I couldn't have done it. Thank you to the Police, the counsellors, the lawyers and the judge for having my back.

To the man who did this, I hope that the time you have spent at counselling/psychologists, the sentence you received, and your baby girl shake you to your core and change your soul to provide the world with a better man then you were two years ago.

His sentence was 18 months with a mandatory 3 months imprisonment, meaning the remaining 15months is on parole.

Neil:

Shit happens! Everyone must go through issues during their life. Nobody has a life of smooth sailing full of only happy smiles and roses.

But there is a difference between us as humans – it is how we choose to deal with moments in our lives. Do we wish to be negative or positive? Do we wish to be confident or scared? My confidence has grown through my international performing on TV shows, experiencing the pressure of being positive enough to succeed and not fail. Also, business decisions, to remain positive that it will work and not fail.

Life is too short to be negative, it's not worth it, and I can't be bothered with it the older I get, including the people I choose to be around. And the older I get, I realise the importance of social interconnectedness as humans for good health. Isolation is not healthy most of the time - not for too long anyway.

During the years of not addressing the issue of abuse, I did a sterling job at ignoring it and pretending it didn't happen. This was my way of trying to be positive and not negative. However, it did need to be addressed and I applied a positive mental attitude in the hope that a positive result was the outcome. And guess what? It worked. Like life, when we have a positive attitude with an intention of a positive result, it is amazing how many times it will result in your favour, may take a few or many goes but it will work out. Go for it.

Heather:

If I could say one thing to somebody to help them on that even just that first step. It's okay, take a breath, open your mouth and let the words come out.

John:

Don't forget to breathe. That means stop and take a breath. Slow down. Take it easy. Take one step before you take the next. And above all be patient.

After I decided to take steps to get better from the challenges it didn't happen the next day. After a year of feeling like nothing was getting better I remember I was drumming my fingers anxiously on a table top quietly resenting that I wasn't feeling change. As I drummed my fingernails on that table I heard the sharp report of fingernail on wood. I lifted my hand and looked at the fingernails that were making the sound and they really needed cutting. That had never happened before. I had always nervously chewed my fingernails to the point that they regularly bled. Over the preceding months they had grown. Without noticing the change, I had a physical manifestation that change was occurring, I just hadn't noticed.

"For intimacy between two people to be truly divine, both must be <u>fully</u> present and surrendered to the other in love, anything less is a heinous act of hate".

-Petros 'The Human GPS' Galanoulis.

The 3 C's of appropriate sexual contact: A straight forward guide and great family discussion point

It's strange to imagine that with all our evolution as human beings and all we have achieved as humans and in today's day an age that we would need to have a guide for people around appropriate sexual conduct.

Yet there seems to be an ignorance, rightly, wrongly its irrelevant, we need to build understanding and have discussions around these. These discussions would be educational, explorative and ensuring that our kids, our future leaders and ourselves men and women know what is acceptable and what is not.

With this in mind I gave some thought to what constitutes appropriate sexual contact and how can I put it in to a simple formula that is easy to understand and to recall and execute. It is with these elements I give to you the **3 C's of appropriate sexual contact…**

1. **C**oherence- one is mentally and emotionally competent and conscious and able to understand and be able to decide and determine for themselves and free from any influences such as drugs, alcohol or threat or any other limiting mental and cognitive state or condition.

2. **C**onsent- One fully and truly gives their consent of their own free will and not through any manipulation or pressuring or other influence etc.

3. **C**o-enjoyment- Something that perhaps does not get looked at or talked about much at all and that is, it's important both parties genuinely enjoy whatever act is being partaken in. It's not enough just for one person enjoying themselves and the other performing out of a sense of obligation or not wanting to disappoint. If its established one party doesn't like what's been done, then cease that act.

This is a great guide for helping someone to behave sexually appropriate and to also discuss at the dinner table both the adults amongst themselves and with their children (when age appropriate) about sex and appropriateness. This is planting the seed for a future with at least reduced sexual transgressions.

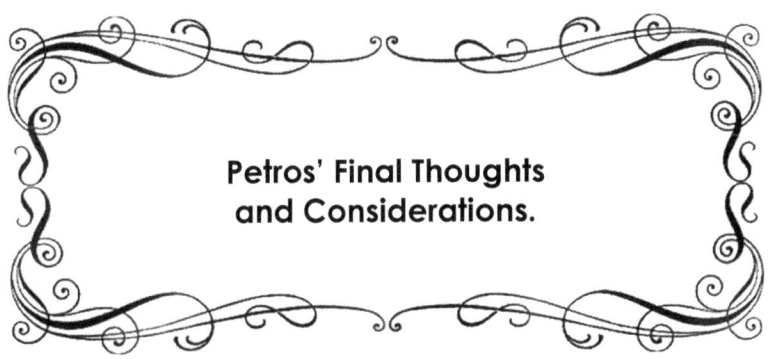

Petros' Final Thoughts
and Considerations.

GIFT 1: FREE FOR YOU ONLINE PROGRAM:

4 Fun Steps To Overcoming The Doldrums.

We all hit a plateau in our life, connect with your creative and authentic self and in 4 fun steps create, map out and action the next phase of your life. Be it a full major new chapter or just a minor direction adjustment.

Plus

GIFT 2: FREE ACCESS-MASIVELY IMPROVE YOUR MINDSET IN 30 DAYS:

30 Day Beat The Blues Challenge.

Do it on your own, with a friend or in a group, even at work. The 30 Day Beat The Blues Challenge is designed for you to take on simple but highly effective and specifically chosen tasks over a 30 day period. The sole purpose and aim of this challenge is to help you improve your mindset, for with an improved mindset comes improved outlook, improved decision making and therefore improved outcomes. You to can be manifesting greater results for you 30 days from now, start today.

Go to: www.yougotthismentalhealth.com.au/bonuses

GIFT 3: 2 COMPLIMENTARY TICKETS

Events by Petros (You Got This: Mental Health Services) are informative, empowering, practical and relevant.

You and a friend are invited to a non-workshop event and its Petros' shout.

With topics such as:

-Beating Panic Brain

-3 Common things you do normally that you shouldn't do when

-having experienced a crisis or trauma

-7 Steps to overcoming a crisis faster and better.

Use coupon code: RFTLBOOK on an eligible event you want to see. To be notified of upcoming events register through below link:

Go to: www.yougotthismentalhealth.com.au/events

*"Too many look towards the end of a journey
and miss all the treasures within it"*

-Petros 'The Human GPS' Galanoulis.

The human journey is an amazing one, it's something that's had me enthralled from a young age, how do we go from a pin head sized drop of fluid to an intricate, conscious intelligent being such as the one you see in the mirror and all around you? Where does the consciousness that drives the vessel that is our body come from and how great is it?

This is a pivotal question, especially that last bit about how great is this intelligent consciousness that drives us, and I believe the only thing more amazing than the human journey is the human spirit as I call it, that drives us through whatever this life has in store for us.

The human spirit is the collective tool box our soul armed itself with when it agreed to take on this life, this form, the main staples of that tool box are first and foremost *Love*, then followed by *Understanding, compassion, resilience, courage, evolvement and forgiveness*. Maybe more can be added and maybe some can be deemed one and the same but its neither here nor there, the above in some way make up the tool box that lies within all of us and available to all of us.

So, what is there to know from all this, here is a most difficult concept and truth (in my opinion) ~ *All events are neutral, they are simply the unfolding of life, the only thing that gives meaning to anything is our perception of it, our beliefs and prejudices, our culture and the conclusions we draw and from that the decisions we make about something.*

This can be quite a tough cookie to swallow but consider for a moment what other truth this also gives light to, we have more power and ability than we know. Taking this human form, we forget our true capability, even though we see it, even if in glimpses throughout our life, part of our journey is to discover our true power in the context of the human experience, to truly know ourselves at the divine level.

How so? No doubt there are few who would disagree rape and sexual assault and other acts of this kind are wrong and awful to say the least, for most people we are able to determine it goes against our divine nature,

However what we see throughout this book and with many outside of the book who have been through such an ordeal, they wouldn't change a thing because of where it had lead them today and this is what I mean by we are more powerful than we realise and it takes events like these sometimes to help us break through to a level of existence we previously could not imagine, a positive existence at that.

If we understand that everything that's happening is the unfolding of life then we can look at things from a more empowering perspective, one that says; 'What happened to me was awful, *in fact it exceeds my current level to understand why something like this happens but that does not by some default mean my life is over or that I allow this event(s) to end my life, my ability to experience something great in this life including forgiveness'.*

When at this point; what you find yourself at is a crisis, now the true definition of a crisis is to be at a turning point, a bend in the road or a fork in the road where you have the power of choice, the power to choose what becomes of you after such a trauma, and awful act.

You could say grief from an event may never actually go away, for that to happen I think the event itself would have to be erased from your life and all emotions and feelings would have to be removed with it and that is not possible. What does happen though in my opinion is as we grow and regain our power, our strength, it becomes easier to handle, manage and live with the grief, we grow if we choose to.

Please be clear, I am not here to justify such acts or to in anyway condone them, I am saying two things here, we may not necessarily control what happens to us externally but we can certainly control and give power to what happens to us internally, and which turn we take in a crisis, secondly these acts, as abhorrent as they are, can serve a positive purpose that hopefully can lead to better understanding which is great for the personal journey and also for the goal of at least reducing such incidents and helping to heal from them better.

You are not what happens to you, you are that which you come away from after a life experience, and that power lies entirely in your hands. You never have to be alone, you are never without resources, and what happened to you does not need to take over you, not permanently, it comes down to one thing~ **_You must decide what will become of you moving forward!_**

A BIG THANKS ONCE AGAIN!

Before I sign off, I would like to give the biggest thanks once again to The Warriors and The redeemed Soul for their willingness to share openly their experiences in my book.

Without them this book would be nothing short of a wishful thought, thank you guys.

Thank you,
Petros 'The Human G.P.S.' Galanoulis

"One is not defined by how many times they fall, instead they are defined by how many times they get back up, even in the face of feeling weak and vulnerable."

-Petros 'The Human GPS' Galanoulis.

About the Author

Petros is a Personal Crisis coach/ counsellor helping people solve and recover mentally and emotionally form a personal trauma and or crisis. He owns and runs *You Got This - Mental Health* services. He is also the author of the nationally acclaimed: *You Got This: 7 Steps to Effectively Solving Any Personal Crisis Better, Faster.*

Based in Melbourne Australia he is referred to as the Human G.P.S. because of his style of coaching and guidance. He works as a Crisis and Trauma Recovery Coach/Counsellor, predominantly with individuals who are struggling through a major and difficult life transition/ event such as post trauma stress, life transitions or loss etc.

Petros also works with organisations and their leadership teams to help them be a positive influence and to know what to do when a staff member is experiencing a personal trauma/ crisis.

With over 15-years of professional experience and over 30-years of personal experience, he developed his coaching process: the G.P.S. system.

Petros holds a diploma in life coaching/ counselling and is completing his university studies in psychology where he has received significant credits and acknowledgment for his work and study done already in mental health. He has also studied the spiritual philosophy of Vedanta and is a Reiki, Hypnotherapy and N.L.P. qualified practitioner.

Petros has appeared in the media, his personal and professional mission is to help as many people he can to **live like they mean it!!**

Petros is also a practical and inspirational speaker and (sometimes cheeky) thought provoker, always exploring the flipside of life with such topics as:

✓ Breaking through 'Panic Brain'

✓ 3 Major actions to take when hit by a crisis

✓ 3 Common things you do normally that you shouldn't do when having experienced a crisis or trauma

✓ 7 effective steps to navigate through any crisis successfully

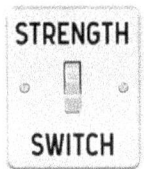

Flip The Switch-10 Week Resilience program is about helping you breakthrough a personal crisis whilst improving resilience and building coping skills, so you can start thriving often. (Done via weblink)

I know all too well the mental and physical toll when your thoughts are going one hundred miles an hour at night and you can't sleep. The shame you can feel when you struggle with simple tasks and functionality because you are sabotaged by anxiety and overwhelm, depression or a lack of knowing what to do.

I have also experienced the frustration of seeing others succeed wildly despite having done less than me and being annoyed that it's not me winning.

The **Flip The Switch-10 Week Resilience program** is designed to take you through the full GPS process and to help breakthrough some of the deeper, more stubborn and longest running mental health issues or mental vandals, be it trauma from childhood, work or family, anxiety, depression, sexual or physical trauma or just feeling stuck and held back in your life. Over a 10-week period you are guided through to work on understanding causes and or triggers, work through them and gain new proactive perspective, we then work on developing a desirable future or outcome to gravitate to...

You will positively experience 8 steps over 7 weeks that will focus on:

1. Pre-Cautions
2. Gathering your bearings-Giving shape to your situation
3. Surveying your territory-Assessing the situation
4. Mapping the situation-Breaking the situation down to see it better
5. Find your best path, creating and assessing options
6. Clear a way forward-Create a desired outcome/ destination to gravitate towards
7. Set your targets, build a plan and strategy and start moving'
8. Arrive at desired outcome, condition mental skills to make it to where you want and be able to cope and repeat in future

BONUS: Followed by 3 weeks of follow-up support counselling via web link.

Once you have gone through this you will have, amongst many other things dealt with or managing much better the crisis that was destroying your happiness and functionality, built a strategy to achieve a greater life for yourself, all the while also building resiliency and coping skills for future challenges and for better, faster healing and thriving in no matter what you do.

To book in or for any questions contact us at:

www.yougotthismentalhealth.com.au/flicktheswitch

**Join Us For Exclusives In
The Reaching For The Light Facebook Group**

Share your favourite parts of the book

Your inspiring story

Support

Great interviews

Insightful and exciting videos.

Events.

Competitions.

Specials plus more.

www.facebook.com/groups/reachingforthelight

For business, collaboration, service or media
enquiries you can find Petros Galanoulis at:

yougotthismentalhealth.com.au/media-and-speaking

OTHER BOOKS BY PETROS GALANOULIS

Petros' first contribution to the literary and personal development sphere is:

You Got This-7 Steps To Effectively Solving Any Crisis Faster, Better.

I share my story and my G.P.S. system, I let you in on my own derailing and how I got back on track, how I found my authentic self and rebuilt my life.

The book comes with over $50 worth of FREE audios and inside the book you will also find many practical activities designed to give you real time results for real life....Your life!

To access this, and more, go to:

www.yougotthismentalhealth.com.au/my-books

CPSIA information can be obtained
at www.ICGtesting.com
Printed in the USA
BVHW091356020119
536867BV00019B/324/P